POWER PLAY

Who's In Control
of the Energy Revolution?

POWER PLAY

Who's In Control
of the Energy Revolution?

by
J. C. Whorton, Jr. and Paulette Whitcomb

This book is dedicated to all the dinosaurs who made it possible, both living and extinct.

Copyright © 1998 by

PennWell Publishing Company

1421 South Sheridan Road/P.O. Box 1260

Tulsa, Oklahoma 74101

```
Whorton, J. C.
    Power play : who's in control of the energy revolution? / by J.C.
  Whorton, Jr. and Paulette Whitcomb.
       p.    cm.
    Includes index.
    ISBN 0-87814-748-9
    1. Energy industries--United States.   I. Whitcomb, Paulette.
  II. Title.
  HD9502.U52W5   1998
  333.79'0973--dc21                                        98-8035
                                                              CIP
```

Printed in the United States of America

1 2 3 4 5 02 01 00 99 98

TABLE OF CONTENTS

FOREWORD

I am president of a commodity exchange that has traded wheat futures for more than 140 years. Nearly three years ago, we entered the energy field when we introduced a Western natural gas contract.

My need for a crash course on the natural gas industry was critical, and I had extreme difficulty in piecing such a course together. So I called on industry leaders such as J.C. Whorton, Jr.,and Paulette Whitcomb for the insight and content needed to help insure the success of our fledgling contract. Since that time, with the advent of electricity's restructuring, the energy industry has become even more complex, not simpler. Thus I was thrilled when J.C. sent me an advance manuscript of *Power Play*. J.C.'s and Paulette's fascinating and comprehensive journey through the energy industry's colorful and storied past proved to be the answer to my fondest hopes for my continued education in a world of energy convergence and ongoing evolution.

This book has all the intrigue and excitement of a darn good novel, and yet it gives the reader a wonderful overview of a wild, sometimes wacky, but truly vital American industry. The best part of the book is that it is written by two longtime participants and keen observers of the industry who do not have any axe to grind or position to sell. They simply tell it like it is, and when the reader realizes how it is, adjectives like *fascinating, unbelievable* and even *scary* come to mind.

This is a book for the seasoned energy veteran, for the rookie just entering some phase of the industry, and for anyone who wants to read an exciting book about a basic American business.

I am proud of my friendship with J.C. and Paulette, and I am truly excited about *Power Play*. I know every reader will share my enthusiasm for the book when they complete "the Trip."

Michael Braude
President and Chief Executive Officer
Kansas City Board of Trade
Kansas City, Missouri
May 1998

PREFACE

I was very fortunate to have begun my energy career as a petroleum landman–a leasehound, as the early-day oil men labeled the profession.

This chosen profession came after very impressionable stints as an officer in the U.S. Army during a very turbulent era and almost four years on the Oklahoma City Police Department covering a myriad of assignments that only reinforced my worst suspicions: *Law enforcement paid union, crime paid market!*

What I appreciated most about being a landman was the privilege of dealing with everyone involved in the exploration and production (E&P) chain–the upstream process. I'm proud to say that even though I attended law school, the ethics of my landman profession (as well as the sheer greed of the energy go-go days unfolding before me) forced me to drop out. Being a landman reinforced my beliefs that my chosen profession was the most glamorous one that could possibly exist without getting shot at on a regular basis.

No other profession offered the opportunity to negotiate in smoke-filled bars, display credible amounts of optimism in the presence of bankers, fight for record books in crowded courthouses, pry for information around bustling drilling rigs, haggle for drilling rights around kitchen tables, testify as to the most just and prudent practice before regulatory agencies–all to produce a unit of energy for the American public.

Oh yeah–and hopefully, to make money.

• • •

As a result of these experiences and many others along the way–I have managed corporations, marketed hydrocarbons, traded commodities, consulted, and lectured–I wish to offer an objective roadmap for use in finding and extracting the ultimate value out of the converging BTU stream and an opportunity to better understand what vision must exist for this new world order.

For me to guide you through the new BTU world, I must shed the excess baggage of biases gathered over three decades. The upstream world of the oil patch in the early days and its founders is all but gone. Many of them, however, still race across the boundaries of my memories and ignite my imagination. Their imprints will be with me forever. I worry that their tomorrows will never be as good as their yesterdays.

The midstream infrastructure that moves the hydrocarbons, as well as its industry leaders, is also aging quickly; like the upstream world, the midstream world is in a critical stage in its evolutionary process. The downstream world now possesses the new blood and ideas.

While these new revolutionaries may have the vision, they do not fully comprehend the legacy. Life in the hydrocarbon world is no longer survival of the biggest or strongest; it has become survival of the leanest and smartest. The security provided by the age-old walls of the regulatory battlements is crumbling. Hydrocarbon Man's legacy is a graveyard of various and colorful styles.

Few will truly miss him. I will never forget him.

J. C. Whorton, Jr.

Evergreen, Colorado

Don Hart has to take all the blame for turning a perfectly lovely human being into an energy and finance writer, editor, and publisher.

In August 1981, he published the premiere issue of a glossy, expensive monthly magazine named *Oil and Gas Investor*, which was adamantly *not* intended to be yet another magazine for the oil-patch trade. The primary reader was to be the investor. The visionary mission of the magazine was to explain the oil and gas industry to this individual so he could make money, or at least not lose it. The industry would of course come to rely on the magazine to see how it was being presented to the investment community and to learn what the latter expected of the industry.

And Hart hired me precisely because I had never worked in the oil patch. He figured I'd learn fast and would help shape the magazine into a vehicle for analyzing the oil patch in lucid, accurate, irreverent, and elegant

English. And I did, I did—I even wrote the much-reprinted *Glossary of Petrolese.*

Seventeen years and one huge oil-patch bust later, *Oil and Gas Investor* is going strong.

Moi? I'm still explaining the industry. This time around it's to a totally different audience, however.

Early on in my career in publishing, I determined never to preach to the choir, but rather to always look for the audience who doesn't even know that it doesn't know. With that in mind, I started up several innovative publications, and each time the audience responded enthusiastically. Astonishing, how quickly people welcome a source of useful information and analysis.

So, fast-forward to 1998: Who needs to have energy deregulation dissected and explained? Not the deregulators and not the regulators—but those who've been sitting there lulled into dreamland by the choir and who are just waking up to realize that the music is beautiful, but they just may be missing something big going on somewhere outside.

I don't know where my career would have headed had I not had the good fortune to get to know an industry of such vitality and power. I do know, however, that I feel very strongly about the need for the U.S. electorate to start making intelligently informed decisions about its energy future. And I would not have taken the time and effort that went into this book if I did not believe that today's electorate is capable of stirring, informing itself, and taking appropriate action to channel what has become the life force of our civilization.

Paulette Whitcomb
Columbine, Colorado

Note: Throughout the book, the word man and the masculine pronouns are used. This usage is for convenience. No sexism is remotely intended. One of the two authors is a woman and proud and happy to be one.

ACKNOWLEDGMENTS

F irst, we need to thank Bob Beck, editor of *Oil & Gas Journal*, who grabbed the manuscript of this book and passed it on to his PennWell colleague Kirk Bjornsgaard, the enterprising acquisitions editor on the book publishing side.

We would like to thank the following energy industry experts for reading the manuscript and providing us with the benefit of their accumulated experience and wisdom: William Bauch, senior vice president, CIBC Oppenheimer, Houston; Michael Braude, president and CEO, Kansas City Board of Trade; Nancy W. George, vice president-governmental relations, El Paso Energy Corp., Washington, D.C.; Susan Steiger Klann, *Oil and Gas Investor* contributing editor and *Denver Post* energy columnist; Ken Nichols, principal, Nichols Consulting, Boulder, Colorado; Dan L. Sanford, attorney-at-law, Verner, Lippfert, Bernhard, McPherson, and Hand Chartered, Washington, D.C.; and Ray Singleton, president, Basic Earth Science Systems, Inc., Denver.

In addition, we would like to acknowledge the assistance of several civilians (as it were)–individuals ranging in age from the World War II generation to Generation X: Carlos E. Milner, Jr., with decades of international experience in hard-rock mining and the computer world, and young professionals Jeffery and Jennifer Fugita, Matthew S. Whitcomb, and Robert and Isabel Zimmerman and university students Jennifer W. Whorten and John C. Whorton. Their reading and criticism of the manuscript helped us in our attempt to make this book meaningful to the BTU consumer outside the energy industry.

In closing, we wish to express our gratitude to our respective spouses, Kimberly Ann Whorton and George H. Whitcomb, who humorously indulged our flamboyantly obnoxious working habits, as they have for decades. Special thanks go to George for providing research assistance and valuable counsel above and beyond the bonds of matrimony and friendship.

And last but not least, our thoughts go to the Lazy W Ranch at the foot of Mount Justice, and to all the critters whose presence inspired and entertained us in our writing: all the horses; Smokey Joe and Sammie Sue, the dogs; Ernest and Homer, the goats, and the Mount Evans Elk Herd (about which, more will be written in our next endeavor).

INTRODUCTION

Change is neither bad nor good, but merely inevitable. What is bad or good is how we manage change. If our society allows change to occur without analysis, without appropriate and thought-out controls, change can do us all irreparable harm, at least until a generation that is bitten to the quick assesses the damage and tries to undo it.

This book involves itself with a most far-reaching change, that occurring in the world of energy as monopolies give way to free markets. Energy has become an intrinsic part of everybody's life, to the point that whoever controls energy has the potential to control society.

Every thinking member of U.S. society at this time needs to decide how to manage the New World of energy before it manages society. To do that requires an understanding of events and their roots, since one can't manage what one doesn't understand. It is, however, an unfortunate fact that the typical member of our society does not really know much about, let alone understand the ongoing changes in the energy world.

Why hasn't the U.S. public of the 1990s been paying attention?

Some answers spring to mind.

- The United States is the most advanced industrialized country on the planet and its citizens view energy, generically speaking, not only as a birthright but almost as a benevolent natural force about which they need not concern themselves.

- Natural gas and electricity have been tightly regulated for so long that, again, the typical American figures those agency bureaucrats have any potential problems covered.

- Many Americans see the world of oil as evil, and see no point in devoting time to understanding it because the villains who run it will always get away with nefarious doings.

- It's a big country with so much going on, nobody has enough time, and things always work themselves out.

- And anyway, energy is highly technical and totally boring.

Is this too cynical a view? We hope so.

But whether it's true of most of the U.S. public or of only a part, the point is that awareness and involvement must replace complacency and inattention. But why are we asking you to fix what ain't broke? After all, the infrastructure hums safely in place; for the most part, reliability of service is not an issue at this time.

We ask because the system itself, and those who run it, are being challenged.

• • •

George Santayana (yes, the fellow who said, "Those who cannot remember the past are condemned to repeat it") wrote in 1920: "All his life the American jumps into the train after it has started and jumps out before it has stopped; and he never once gets left behind or breaks a leg."

That may have been true at the time. It probably won't work today. The stakes are much higher and the train's going a whole lot faster. This is a good time to make up our minds that learning about the energy upheaval all around us is most definitely in our job description. You know–that being-a-good-citizen thing.

The new energy value stream–the so-called BTU value stream–is central to our national security, our economy, and the very nature of our industrial infrastructure. Every man, woman, and child in North America is a participant in this stream. Innovation and technology are constantly remaking our world, but since there are just so many issues the mind can absorb, we tend to lose sight of the interrelationships and the consequences. But if you don't understand the issues, you can't pick a side–and then a side picks you, because in a revolution, "not playing" is not an option. You are part of a

$300-billion war. This is not Monopoly money we're playing with here.

This book is for you, the energy participant, as you start on the Energy Revolution journey.

You're paying for the trip, so wouldn't you like to be involved in the planning process? You know–decide where you want to end up? At this point, your tour guide has been scouting you for a long time, through all the previous deregulatory experiences. He expects you to just go along for the ride. You did before, after all. For the playing field to be level, it's imperative for you to do some scouting of your own.

• • •

We begin by outlining the evolutionary beginnings of today's revolution, and then describing the revolutionaries, their motives, and how they will profit. We introduce you to the Time Bandits and ask you to reflect on how much competition you truly need and how much choice you can really afford.

We explore the new player created by the revolution–the Marketer as the Re-Marketer. We take a look at several Unintended Consequences of deregulation in a number of other industries and ponder that uncomfortable corollary of Murphy's Law: "Mother Nature always sides with the hidden flaw."

In the spirit of the French proverb, "The more it changes, the more it becomes the same," we ask: If the free market that follows the breakup of monopoly becomes so cutthroat that smaller competitors fall by the wayside, does consolidation into a few major players eventually lead us back into the monopoly we scrapped in the first place?

We see the public utilities facing radical reformation as they struggle with competitors not shackled by regulatory constraints. The utility as you know it today simply will not survive, and neither will its regulatory agency; the deregulation of other industries provides insights that cannot be ignored.

While the issue of control is central to this book, we ask you to consider that most difficult kind of control–the kind not exercised from the top down but rather exercised by us all as collectively involved consumers. Who, for instance, should be better motivated to control today's public company than its shareholder? And that shareholder is you, because even if you don't have thousands of shares of energy companies in your portfolio, odds are that your qualified pension plan or life insurance policy does. Certainly *someone* is empowered.

When you do nothing, you allow someone else to do something. The current trend is the abdication of control in favor of the emerging czar of the street–the corporate analyst.

We take a long look at the energy merchants and the energy players and ask: What new opportunities or choices is the revolution bringing to these two sectors? What changes? What fads? What trends? What new risks?

To manage change and its associated financial risks, many energy companies are forced to utilize arcane financial tools such as derivatives–arcane in that they are understood by few, especially senior management and boards of directors. The unintended consequences of companies attempting to be risk-averse and inadvertently stepping on financial land mines are grim reminders. (Remember Orange County and Barings Bank?) Each energy company is trying to choose the migration path most appropriate to its needs in a quickly shifting landscape.

It's a world in which value streams from crude oil and its refined products, natural gas, coal, hydro, nuclear, and electricity, merge into the BTU value stream. We focus primarily on oil and its refined products here, and on natural gas, as these will most likely have an immediate impact on the consumer.

These separate and tightly compartmentalized industries are now headed for *convergence*. Using the definition offered by international consulting firm Hagler Bailly, convergence means that "instead of purchasing gas, electricity, water, cable, and telecommunications services discretely, consumers will soon select bundles of infrastructure services, customized to meet their individual needs. Business and market drivers are spurring convergence in the provision of such infrastructure services."

Today, yesterday's "discretely operating industries" are not only merging but hopefully cross-pollinating, despite obstacles such as corporate egos, a generation skip, and loss of legacy, as well as the widespread misuse of forecasting and thoughtless disregard of its built-in flaws.

And because we're all adults here, we have to recognize the existence of certain spin doctors and immutable personality types who predate the revolution and will undoubtedly outlast it. They have a powerful effect on events, yet their nature is such that nobody can exercise much control over them. However, the consumer–a.k.a. the U.S. public, the aware citizen–can at the very least learn to recognize the temperaments and mindsets involved, and thus not be lured or misled by their mind games and agendas. Forewarned is forearmed.

There is history in this book, along with a great deal of personal observation and experience, some biases, and considerable projection. There are a great many questions–more questions than answers. We trust that this book will stir you into providing a lot of the answers or, at the very least, into helping to enact some of the new rules. Before anyone springs into action, however, it's vital to understand the issues and events unfolding across this continent.

We have tried to offer not only insight, but also a useful perspective on the new energy world as it affects our lives. In order to coexist intelligently and responsibly as the markets evolve, the consumer and the energy player need to clarify their individual roles and determine appropriate controls. This book brings both sides to the table in an attempt to replace the adversarial relationship of the past with a realization that they must interact with each other as equals because each has what the other needs.

The nonenergy reader gets a behind-the-scenes look at a very powerful and inbred industry and its roots, the energy world's basic realities. The energy reader gets the opportunity to revisit the forces that have shaped his image, to consider his emerging identity, and to acknowledge that the consumer's need and want for the commodity is the vehicle that drives him to market.

This is neither a trader's how-to guide nor an academician's treatise. This is a fact-based, hands-on narrative of unabashed, possibly politically incorrect opinions. We have enjoyed writing it, and we hope you will enjoy thinking your way through it.

Let's now take the first step of our journey into the past and future of the BTU world.

SECTION I: GETTING READY FOR THE TRIP

ROADMAP TO THE REVOLUTION

"A funny thing happened on the way to the forum."

—Burt Shevelove and Larry Gelbart

Y ou say you haven't noticed a revolution going on. No blood in the streets, no visible property damage, no wrenching disruption of services…

Yes, it is a quiet revolution, isn't it? But a revolution all the same. The reason you haven't noticed it—the reason that the media plays up the latest murder and sports upset and stuffs the revolution in the business news section—is quite simple: The revolution did not start with wild-eyed malcontents at the grassroots. This revolution started in boardrooms, not tenements. The agitators were at the top; most of their demands have already become the law of the land in the hallowed name of market competition, consumer choice, and lower prices for all.

The revolution has already affected society from the grassroots on up, and its effects are accelerating. But most Americans don't think of it as a revolution, if they think of it at all.

Those who have given some thought to the energy world of the 1990s tend to view its change simply as the breaking up of energy monopolies, the opening up of choices, and the falling prices that accompany free-market competition. That is a true part of the picture, but only a part.

The reason that the changes in the world of energy spell revolution, despite the lack of bloodshed and chaos, is that their effects on today's America–industrial, commercial, residential, social, and political, from Wall Street to Main Street–are causing a paradigm shift as radical as if armed bands roamed your neighborhood. The end result will be one of the most radical transformations of the industrial-commercial economic base and regulatory infrastructure this country has ever seen.

The regulated monopolies were put in place not to restrict competition, but to protect the resources and the process from the robber barons–from producer through to end-user and investor. Regardless of good intentions, however, it is a fact that as long as a monopoly exists, those outside the monopoly are stuck outside the money machine. The only way to get at it is to convince the government to break up the monopoly, and to convince the customer he needs the choices and the less-expensive goods allegedly always born out of competition.

But as today's revolutionaries penetrate the energy monopolies–as the title of this book suggests–the basic question is, *Who's in control?*

Energy is, today more than ever, the ultimate source of all power–physical, economic, and political. The revolution has been shifting the controls of this enormous engine away from traditional hands to a new set of hands. The new marketers believe it's their hands, but the controls are actually in the hands of all of us as consumers and taxpayers if we choose to exercise them.

We can't handle the controls if we can't even find the revolution.

So let's go find it, shall we?

FIRST CAME EVOLUTION

How did this energy revolution get started?

As noted previously, in the boardrooms. It started in the natural gas industry. Once upon a time, not very long ago, natural gas was a tightly regulated industry in which the pipelines held sway. Those at the wrong end of the food chain—the producers—and those totally outside the food chain—the would-be gas marketers—wanted a crack at the moneymaking game that the pipelines controlled absolutely. They lobbied. Their rallying cry was *competition*—open up the markets and offer everybody the lower prices that competing in an open market would naturally bring.

It worked, but most Americans did not notice because as long as their gas is there when they turn it on, the process *per se* does not hold their attention. In any case, the process of natural gas deregulation was evolutionary.

The first big step in the process came in 1985, with action by the Federal Energy Regulatory Commission (FERC). The FERC is a quasi-independent agency within the U.S. Department of Energy having jurisdiction over interstate electricity sales, wholesale electric rates, hydroelectric licensing, natural gas transmission, and related services such as pricing, gas pipeline certification, and oil pipeline rates. The FERC issued Order 436, which required pipeline companies to open access to the pipes.

The next big step, Order 636, in 1992, was momentous. Pivotally, 636 reduced the pipelines to mere carriers and basically said that anybody anywhere could sell natural gas to anybody—producer directly to end-user, producer to marketer, producer or marketer to pipeline.

The winners were those wise enough to recognize the opportunities provided by open access when it was allowed to operate all across the value stream—the real beginning of today's convergence. The losers were those who lost the keys to the money machine because they took the path of denial rather than that of acceptance, repositioning, and transformation—the path that leads to growth.

The energy media covered this evolution like a wet blanket but, for the most part, the consumer media yawned. Unless consumers wanted to plow through the energy magazines, newspapers, and newsletters (with an interpreter of the technical, regulatory, and financial jargon at their sides), they left it alone.

Understandable. After all, *revolutions* get a lot of attention. *Evolutions* just sort of drift along without prime-time speeches. No one ever sculpts heroic statues of famous "evolutionaries" to place proudly in front of public buildings. Nor does anyone excite followers into action with great battle cries like, "Give me slow and steady evolution, or I'll quietly go away." And when an evolution deals with something like natural gas, it's as quiet as a baby growing hair. The family notices every strand; the neighborhood may notice if baby's still bald when he turns three.

Those who had agitated for the deregulation of natural gas moved quietly but very quickly. Remember, it was the FERC that guided the process of deregulating the natural gas industry–paradoxically, a governmental body and its various commissioners through the years gave away most of their authority and replaced it with market forces, a unique act for a bureaucratic body. Only in America.

And a uniquely American type of hard-driving entrepreneur seized the opportunity to turn the once-shackled energy molecule into profit. Chuck Watson of Natural Gas Clearinghouse (now NGC Corporation), Oscar Wyatt of Coastal, Charles Koch of Koch Industries, Cortland Dietler of Associated Natural Gas (now part of Duke Energy Corp.), and others wasted no time pondering the philosophy that impelled (and still impels) the FERC on its course toward "unbundling" the energy markets and freeing industry from artificially high costs. They acted in their best self-interest.

In so doing, they shaped a new market. They changed the financial markets' focus from London, New York, Paris, and Hong Kong to such well-known natural gas trading centers as Muddy Creek, Waha, Henry Hub, Sumas and Empress, Leidy, and Ventura. In so doing, they made the FERC's vision work. Profit-driven visionaries turned out to be the FERC's best friends, in an almost perfect example of American capitalism at its best.

Funny how revolutions start out.

REVOLUTION MARCHES IN

Executives in their boardrooms did not just sit back and admire their newfound natural gas markets. They went for the big one: Electricity.

Back in 1978, in an initial step, the U.S. Congress had passed the Public Utility Regulatory Policy Act (PURPA). Its goals were twofold: Encourage the development of small-scale cogeneration and renewable resources, and apply some competitive pressure on utilities to better control their generating costs. Thus was born the nonutility generating industry, or NUGS, a.k.a. the independent power producers, or IPPs. (The energy field bows to no one in its spawning of acronyms, which is definitely an obstacle for the civilian trying to understand the field.)

The IPPs generated electricity primarily through cogeneration and in regional pockets; still, they had become a competitor for the established utility monopolies. The predators brought increasing pressure to bear. The federal government proved a willing listener. Thus, in 1992–not coincidentally, the same year as Order 636 deregulated the natural gas industry–came the Energy Policy Act (EPACT). This authorized the FERC to permit bulk power trading of electricity at the *wholesale* level. The drumbeat of pressure intensified. In 1995, the FERC issued its outline for restructuring the whole power industry. The final order came in April 1996.

GRAB THAT WHEEL

The revolution had started, and the states, led by California, grabbed the steering wheel. Arizona, Illinois, Massachusetts, New Hampshire, New York, Pennsylvania, Rhode Island, and Wisconsin were among the leaders in changing the face of their retail electric business, either by passing laws or by approving action plans whose common denominator was open supply competition and customer choice.

In New Hampshire, choice took on a Baskin-Robbins flavor, with 31 providers touting their services and vying for the customer's business by offering various come-ons–everything from $50 bills to free bird feeders. (That last come-on is particularly inventive when the customers' electric power goes out and most of what they do grinds to a total halt, at least they can feed the birds and watch them eat–or, in a sustained outage, catch them and eat them.)

Other states continued to follow the lead of these barricade-smashers. The Washington International Energy Group, in Washington, D.C., estimated that by the first quarter of 1997, 43% of the U.S. population lived in states in which customer choice for electricity had been written into law or essentially mandated. (Fig. 1-1)

The movers and shakers in these states suffer from one common ailment, high electricity prices. The cost of 1 kilowatt hour (KWhr) of electric-

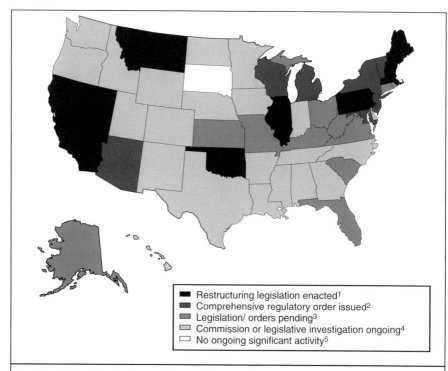

Restructuring legislation enacted[1]
Comprehensive regulatory order issued[2]
Legislation/ orders pending[3]
Commission or legislative investigation ongoing[4]
No ongoing significant activity[5]

[1]California, Illinois, Maine, Massachusetts, Montana, Nevada, New Hampshire, Oklahoma, Pennsylvania, and Rhode Island.
[2]Arizona, Maryland, Michigan, New Jersey, New York, Vermont, and Wisconsin.
[3]Alaska, Connecticut, Florida, Kansas, Kentucky, Missouri, Ohio, South Carolina, Virginia, and West Virginia.
[4]Alabama, Arkansas, Colorado, District of Columbia, Delaware, Georgia, Hawaii, Idaho, Indiana, Iowa, Louisiana, Minnesota, Mississippi, Nebraska, New, Mexico, North Carolina, North Dakota,
[5]South Dakota

Source: Energy Information Administration

Fig. 1-1 The status of deregulation of the electric power industry nationwide. (Adapted from Strategic Energy, Ltd.)

ity in the United States averaged 6.9 cents in 1996, but it was very unevenly spread. (Fig. 1-2) In Kentucky, for example, the cost is a tad above 4 cents; in Idaho, it's 3.9 cents. In the New England states, the KWhr cost averages out to 10.3 cents; New York, Illinois, and Michigan averages are also considerably over the national average at 8.0, 7.8 and 7.2 cents, respectively, but California's 9.4 cents have those beat. Nevada, Utah, and Wyoming? Respectively, 5.8, 5.3, and 4.3. Florida is at 7.3 cents, but then Alaska is at 10.2, and Hawaii leads all the states with 12 cents even.

In the states that led the deregulatory charge, legislatures acted in

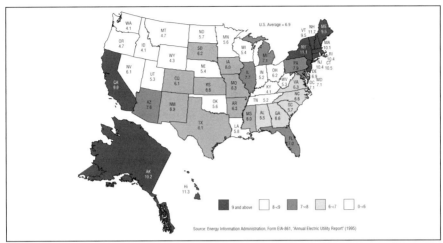

Fig. 1-2 Average revenue from electricity sales to all retail customers by state, 1995 (cents per kilowatt-hour). From Energy Information Agency, Form EIA-861, Annual Electric Utility Report" (1995)

response to the relentless pressure brought to bear by the industrials and larger municipalities who were aggressively chasing lower energy bills–not the residential customers.

Predictably, the U.S. Congress has moved into the battleground, and big money is firing big guns. According to congressional disclosure reports and the nonpartisan Center for Responsive Interest, in Washington, D.C., by year-end 1996 special-interest groups on all sides of the electric-deregulation issue had spent $37 million to lobby Congress and had funneled an additional $11.7 million into PAC contributions.

An excellent illustration of what Congress will typically be considering is the bill proposed by the chairman of the House Commerce Subcommittee on Energy and Power, Rep. Dan Schaefer (R-CO). (While Schaefer has announced that 1998 will be his last year in office, his bill will undoubtedly live on in some form.) In brief, the congressman's Electric Consumers' Power to Choose Act allows any company that wants to generate and/or market electricity to do so. If states have not permitted such competition among power providers by December 15, 2000, the bill empowers the FERC to do it for them.

According to Schaefer, his deregulatory measure will cut the average homeowner's monthly bill of $75 by 20% or more. A hip slogan and 20%

off your electric bill–a slam-dunk combo, right?

Well, Schaefer's bill has run into some stiff opposition. Does this come only from the predictable opponents–the electric utilities, whose monopoly is being gored, or utility shareholders' groups, whose savings (life savings, in many instances) are at stake? No, surprisingly enough, some opposition is coming from the grassroots.

Coming alive to the sound of the big boys' music, residents of most small towns and rural areas point out that they are still waiting to see the blessings promised them by the deregulatory reform of trucking and the railroads, as well as the airlines and telecommunications. Power deregulation, they say, will empower them to try to cut win-win deals with free-market providers who ignore their existence now and can keep right on ignoring their existence.

By way of background, in the same way that motor vehicles and paved roads did, rural electric co-ops started to fill the gap between rural and urban life in the early years of the New Deal. Owned and operated by the people they serve, co-ops provide service in almost every state. Almost all farms now have electric service, compared with 10% when the Rural Electric Administration (REA) was formed in 1935. This social program successfully energized a static lower class.

How will wholesale *and* retail power competition and the loss of subsidies from the REA alter the Norman Rockwell brush strokes of power to rural America?

The rural electric co-ops will very likely get stuck with the responsibility for the truly rural customers–the customers the free-market competitors don't want. Those competitors will most likely cherry-pick the rurals' well-to-do customers–that is, the profit margin. The Rural Electric Administration then becomes the food stamp administration, once again subsidizing rural America.

No, the grassroots aren't marching on Washington, but they're putting up a fight. And environmentalists and consumer groups are joining them in increasing numbers.

So, the revolution is well and truly engaged. Where do you fit in? Right about where your wallet gets picked. Let's see how that is being made to happen.

PAYING FOR THE TRIP

"Just because you're paranoid doesn't mean they aren't out to get you."
—Popular saying

"You pays your money, and you takes your choice."
—From a peepshow rhyme as quoted in *Punch*

H istorically, energy money has flowed into three very separate and distinct value streams.

The *upstream* sector meant exploration and production (E&P) in oil and gas and generation in electricity. The *midstream* sector involved gathering, processing, marketing, storing, and transporting in oil and gas and transmission in electricity. The downstream sector included delivery to the customer, the end-user, the final destination and took the form of oil and gas refining, electricity distribution, and/or merchandising of the finished products.

Money was made all along the value stream until the energy reached its final destination. At that point, the refined product became a service; the demand for that service drove the value stream.

Deregulation–*the essence of the energy revolution*–turned the various forms of energy into pure commodities to be bought and sold in highly competitive and volatile commodity markets, just like hogs and gold. Note that commodity markets are the only places where:

$$1 + 1 = 1$$

That is, to have an open interest, you must have 1 + 1—a long and a short, a winner and a loser. It's a zero sum game: For every winner, there's an equal and proportionate loser.

In addition, deregulation has removed all the locks between the value streams. What used to be slow but sure navigation through the Panama Canal has become the cutthroat ocean race for the America's Cup. In other words, while the revolution has brought opportunities and choices, it has removed protection and intends to continue doing so—but that's for another chapter.

We no longer have individual energy streams—the crude stream, say, or the natural gas stream. The widely accepted name for what we have now is the BTU stream. *BTU* comes from the common abbreviation for British thermal unit—that is, the quantity of heat energy it takes to raise the temperature of one pound of water one degree Fahrenheit, regardless of the source of the heat.

End-users have a choice of energy, a choice of BTU—type. For example, retail consumers have a choice of gas- or electricity-operated appliances; commercial consumers can generate steam from oil, gas, or coal; and all consumers can choose to spend money on energy efficiency, thus reducing their energy expenditures—dealing in negawatts, not megawatts.

Look at a barrel of crude. What do you see? Motion. Look at a cubic foot of natural gas. What do you see? Heat. Now look at a kilowatt of electricity. If you don't see a Technicolor spectrum of needs and desires met, convenience and necessity mingled, the essential and the optional blurred, you don't live in an industrialized society.

So, first we refined the dinosaur into lamp oil; we further refined the monster into motion, then heat. And now that old dinosaur runs our life, our liberty, and the pursuit of our happiness. It hasn't drawn a breath for eons but it's shaping our future. That energy source coming out of the ground has never been static, it has always changed, and now it's controlling time and information.

In any of the industrialized societies, everything done at home, work, or play is dependent upon some form of energy. Energy has become an inelastic commodity, in that we have to have it regardless of its cost. And the more we have, the more we want.

Let's examine a paradox we have all experienced. As our incomes and standards of living rise, our discretionary time does not free up, but rather shrinks to critical supply. It becomes a scarce resource. Our "free" time is far from free; actually, it's getting more expensive by the minute. What do we use to acquire more desperately needed time? Energy.

We use energy more and more not merely to meet basic needs but to *buy time*. We also use energy to buy information—but aren't we repeating ourselves? Today, what is information but another face of time? (You may want to follow the ongoing statistical studies on this subject by Svein S. Andersen and Oystein Noreng of the Norwegian School of Management's Centre for Energy Studies.)

Energy now fulfills a combination of psycho-social-economic wants and needs; the user needs and/or desires a basket of energy products for personal reasons he may only dimly understand or would not care to try to explain in the words of cold reason. Most of us may think logically, but we certainly buy irrationally.

Look at the vehicles we drive. How much of that choice is totally rational? The vehicle dealerships are all too aware of the pickup phenomenon, for example, in which a city-dwelling man with no background in construction or agriculture fulfills some sort of deep psychic need by tooling around in a gas-guzzling vehicle that is almost laughably out of tune with his daily life. And how many well-groomed, exquisitely accoutered dwellers in gated communities in mild-climate regions of the country, whose only outdoor activity is golf, drive in solitary splendor to the office in sport-utility vehicles?

• • •

So, we have a revolution led by a dinosaur, a level landscape where there is no longer controlled obsolescence, because no monopolist controls the market, and everybody can be in the game. And isn't that a wonderful image, an exhilarating concept—the prehistoric past striding into the future, enlightened capitalism triumphant as the mighty stream of united energy values goes rolling along for the heart-warming benefit of everybody, from the producer to the end-user and on to the investor.

Kind of tough on the truly rural customers, the residential customers, and the environment…but, after all, to make an omelet, you have to break eggs, and to make a revolution, you have to break into some wallets.

Surely you don't mind if one of them is yours.

CHOICE–IT'S WHAT YOU ALWAYS WANTED

Those who agitated for the deregulation of electricity–that is, for the opportunity to penetrate the monopoly and be permitted to generate and market electricity–have already penetrated your consciousness.

"Consumer choice" is their core slogan. (Their *official* slogan, that is. Their private slogan is, "Show me your money!") You have noticed the bill-boards, the advertisements, the offers in your mail, the increasing number of corporate mergers and consolidations, and, oh yes, the catchy new logos, like an upside-down E.

The infiltration of infotainment has already begun. Watching the major advertisers for major sporting events, such as the Super Bowl, haven't you wondered, "Who are those guys? What, exactly, are they selling? And why would they pay that much for a 30-second spot?"

Answering the last question first, initial expenditures are inconsequential in light of the enormous profit potential.

"Those guys" are Enron Corporation and a handful of fraternal brothers (Duke Energy, NGC Corp., UtiliCorp, Coral Energy Resources, and El Paso). Then there are all the Enron wannabes. But there's only one Enron, the creation of Ken Lay and his think tank in Houston.

Enron started out just like a lot of other companies. But where others may find profit in refining products, Enron found megabucks in refining markets. The brilliance lies not only in the outside-the-lines thinking: Lay & Co. get it done and make it happen. Enron came off the mark lightning-fast in getting a FERC wholesale power marketer permit. By the time others were applying for their permits, Enron was already moving ahead.

Now you can see Enron on your TV screen as the electrical benefactor of New Hampshire and the Philippines. "Unlike others who say they will build new sources of renewable power *if* customers come, Enron is making that investment today," said Lay in November 1997, as he announced construction of a 39-megawatt wind farm in Southern California that will provide electricity for Enron Earth Smart Power. You can't argue with being on the side of Mother Earth.

Right, but what is the ultimate goal? The one-stop shop, where the customer covers all his energy, telecom, entertainment, and home-security needs by writing one quick check. Sounds reasonable. But let's examine what lies behind the one-stop shop–the tradeoff between you, the new consumer, and this new marketer.

Why is the consumer "new"? Remember, electricity deregulation is the *raison d'être* for the convergence of the various energy streams into the BTU stream. Convergence has created the opportunity for the BTU marketer to bundle various products and thereby satisfy his desire for ever-increasing revenues and market share in hopes that profit will soon follow.

If commodity is the vehicle that drives the marketer to his market–and it is–then the BTU stream is the highway for all the new products and services created by convergence.

Enron & the boys can lead the charge because they have the gas and electricity infrastructure–the physical assets, the marketing advantages, and an inelastic customer base. Not only do they have a commodity to drive, but it's an elastic commodity–that is, a commodity that the customer *has* to have, such as food or shelter, rather than a cellular phone or a home-security system, which are nice items but not vital to survival. This gives them the greatest marketing opportunity of all time: that is, bundling inelastic commodities right along with elastic ones into a menu of services.

Their issue has become: How do we bundle them and remarket them?

The BTU marketer needs a market, so he creates the choice. For the BTU marketer, that one-stop-shop target means total war with his peers. In the consumer-marketing war rooms, relationship marketing teams and the like are spending a lot of money really fast. Just as in a war the combatants can't manufacture planes and tanks fast enough, so it is for the BTU marketers as they fight for market share in the trenches.

Don't mistake this for a choice that you, the new consumer, has asked for. It is the marketers who need the choice. The consumer's only real choice is whom he gets to pay. These are serious bucks–very high stakes. John Olson, the highly respected natural gas analyst for Merrill Lynch & Co., Inc. in Houston, estimates the worth of the retail natural gas/electric market at $300 billion. That is roughly *triple* the size of the market for long-distance communication. If you shudder at how voters are manipulated, it's nothing compared to how manipulated the energy consumer is and will continue to be.

TODAY'S CONSUMER

A marketer either takes to the market what the market wants or makes the market want what he has.

Today's BTU marketer is dealing largely with a consumer who has the following characteristics: He prizes convenience above all else and is willing to pay for it. He's always running out of time and is willing to pay quite handsomely to get some. He has no brand or corporate loyalty. His *me-too* and *right-now* acquisitiveness makes the Sun King at Versailles look like a monk in a cell.

This consumer thinks of himself as a tough customer who knows the score, but in reality he can be easily seduced through his weak spot, which is his visual orientation and Pavlovian reaction to slick packaging and hip presentations. He lives in a society of buzzwords, depends on sound bites for much of his information, and believes CNN is hard, in-depth news. As a result, this pseudo-sophisticate never really knows what he's getting. But if it's packaged slick enough, he'll go for it.

Take salads. It used to be that if we wanted a big, mixed salad, we had to buy three different heads of lettuce plus tomatoes, peppers, radishes, scallions, and carrots. Today's consumers–the nuclear family that eats in shifts, the young singles, the working mothers–are tired of going to a lot of trouble for a lot of waste, all of which takes a lot of time they can't afford, anyway. They've taken to buying take-out salads on their way home from work.

There's a turf war involved here. On the one hand, we have the take-out fast-food establishments and the delis; on the other hand, we have the supermarkets.

How could the latter retain market share, much less hope to increase it? There was no indignant outcry from the American salad-lover–"Give me premixed salad, or I'll boycott your produce aisles!" Time-harried and space-limited consumers just started cutting into the supermarkets' margins by not buying produce in bulk.

So, the produce-industry marketers went to work, and now the consumer can buy at least five different kinds of premixed, packaged salad, from traditional to gourmet, right in the supermarket produce section. The price is not righteous, but the convenience is there for the consumer, and assorted lettuces, half a tomato, a quarter pepper, and three radishes do not lie moldering away in that consumer's crisper. What's more, the supermarkets have a whole new product to help them retain–even increase–market share.

That's what marketers do; that's their job. Whether it's a bunch of scallions or an Mcf of natural gas (see Appendix II), the concept remains the same. Create the choice and/or convenience and margins may follow–at least for a while.

WHAT PRICE CHOICE?

"Even if we *know* that we're being manipulated," you ask, "isn't choice cool? How can it hurt?"

But the relevant question is actually quite different. Ask yourself, "How much choice can we afford?"

Let's look at a classic non-energy example–the proliferation of the so-called "business directories," or what we used to call the Yellow Pages. It's another revolution being waged, allegedly, on your behalf. Any business with goods or services to sell used to willingly advertise in the Yellow Pages.

The cost of their ad was conveniently added to the existing phone bill on a prorated basis.

With Ma Bell's court-ordered breakup and subsequent deregulation, marketers seized the opportunity to create new business directories. They cherry-picked the most lucrative markets (avoiding nonprofitable areas) and blitzkrieged the rest.

Now businesses are compelled to advertise in *all* the directories in order to remain competitive. Choice has become mandatory. Where a business had subscribed for one big ad, maybe even a full-page ad, in the only directory available, that business now places smaller and smaller ads (and, by necessity, more impersonal ones) in order to stretch an ad budget across all the directories. Now he really has no choice but to cave in to every marketer that walks through the door—yet his advertising budget is not very flexible.

The result, then, is what had been an advertisement of choice and a very valuable tool is now an obligation to advertise all across the battleground. The number of directories in which his ad appears has actually divided his advertising exposure. For him the question becomes, "How many marketers can I acquiesce to?"

For you, his potential customer, the questions become, "How many directories will I tolerate? How many variations on the Yellow Pages theme do I need? How many do I have space for?" (Remember, time and space represent money.) "How much time do I want to spend examining all the directories to determine which I keep and use, and which I toss?"

Just as in the energy revolution, the war being fought by the Big Boys is for market share, and not all marketers are going to last. The consumer is a casualty every time he comes home to find ten pounds of directory and thinks he should take the time to make an informed decision as to whether to keep it. (Think—do you know many people who dash off to the local lumberyard to build business-directory library shelves for their homes?) In a body-count directory war, every time the consumer tosses a directory, that marketer becomes a casualty.

And so, here's another revolution you didn't start—but it's one in which someone is constantly grabbing at your watch and your wallet. "Time and space—time to be alone, space to move about—these may well be the greatest scarcities of tomorrow," said Edwin Way Teale in 1956 in *Autumn Across America*. That was two generations ago. Care to rephrase the sentiment for two generations hence?

Remember that true luxury equals as much time and information as you can buy. Perhaps you should consider telling the BTU marketer: "If you inundate me with choice, you're taking my time. You're taking with one hand what you've just given me with the other." There's such a thing as paralysis of analysis.

Quickly, now—a test: Name the five main differences between AT&T, MCI, and Sprint. Don't worry if you get only two correct. You're still ahead of most of your peers.

Once the basic product is the same and the differences between products lie in petty stuff ("petty stuff" that takes hours to study and interpret), the BTU marketer is not making the consumer the gift of choice. No, the BTU marketer has become the thief of time. And today, more than ever before, time is money.

Don't look now, but the guy's picking your wallet and he's already got your watch. These are the revolutionaries with their white hats off. These are the revolutionaries without disguise. These are the Time Bandits.

IT'S NOT THE PRINCIPLE, IT'S THE MONEY

Remember that when you hear, "It's not the money; it's the principle of the thing," you can rest assured—it's the money. Vast amounts of money stand to be made via this revolution. When you see and hear marketers holding principles up for your unquestioning approval as sacred tenets of our republic, you best hide your wallet.

You are being asked to unhesitatingly endorse the concept that the competition born of a free market makes for customer choice, which in its turn makes for lower energy costs. Like all sweeping generalities, this one needs a qualifier or two.

We have already seen how the manic proliferation of choice is going to cost you time and money. There are several significant instances where the ongoing deregulatory moves will *definitely* cost you, or in the best possible scenario, not bring you the promised savings.

The solution to minimizing the depth of the bite? Acquire a thorough understanding of the issues and their genesis.

STRANDED COSTS

This is the big one. The stranded costs issue revolves around utility investments in the range of $200 billion to $400 billion, mostly in the form of generation plants that competition is expected to render too costly for the utility to operate. Most of these are nuclear power plants whose building was heavily financed and remains mostly unretired, to the tune of $89 billion, some experts estimate.

Nuclear or otherwise, these investments are believed to be economically unrecoverable, i.e., stranded. Some utility critics have called these stranded investments "stupid investments." Hindsight is always 20-20, of course. These investments do not represent unilateral decisions by the utilities involved; they were made with regulatory approval. What they really amount to is poor to rotten forecasting decisions—something that has plagued all sectors of the energy industry and the services that support it.

The real issue we need to resolve is the prudence with which the process is executed. Who determines the investments' economic obsolescence? Who is controlling the starter watch and chains? How many of these allegedly stranded investments will resurface in other hands in a deregulated environment? One man's trash is another man's treasure, after all.

You don't have to get involved in the process to insure its prudence, of course. The question, then, is how many bailouts you want to pay for. The S&L bailout was such fun for everybody involved; why don't we do it again? Can't wait for the opportunity to fund another boondoggle like the Resolution Trust Company. (The RTC was a perfect misnomer, as it provided no resolution and inspired no trust.)

For their part, the utilities are pushing for "securitization." This is stranded-cost recovery in the form of an up-front, lump-sum payment to the utility. The customer would fund it through a surcharge that would be a part of his utility bill for 5 to 10 years. Under a securitization scheme, the state legislature or the utility commission would order the customer within the utility's original service territory to pay the surcharge, no matter who supplies electricity to the customer now. That gives *customer choice* a whole new dimension, doesn't it?

It's called securitization because the revenue stream that is expected to come from customer surcharges will be converted into marketable securities–bonds to be issued and sold into the securities markets. Not surprisingly, Wall Street is pushing securitization as hard as the utilities are.

So, let's see, the customer–who has already been paying for assets that may be stranded–pays the utility what the utility paid for the "stranded" assets, plus the costs of maintenance and decommission of those assets. Securitization does not create or destroy wealth; instead, it ensures that the customer, not the utility shareholder, takes the hit, and that the assets stay on the balance sheet. The assets in question are tangible, physical ones that would be fully paid for after the securitization process is complete.

According to IPALCO Enterprises, "If the government had authorized stranded cost recovery for Ford Motor Company's unfortunate decision to market the Edsel, all automobile buyers over a period of years would have had to pay a surcharge to reimburse Ford for the costs incurred in developing and tooling up to produce the Edsel, together with a 'reasonable' return on those investments."

Outside of the utilities and Wall Street, securitization (also euphemistically known as rate-reduction bonds or competitive-transition charges) has met with enormous opposition.

In Michigan, Attorney General Frank J. Kelley has stated, "Only two groups will benefit from issuance of rate reduction bonds: the utility, which will receive the billions in proceeds, and Wall Street, which will receive millions in fees."

The New York General Assembly spearheaded opposition to this recovery scheme. In Texas, this one issue brought down the bill designed to open competition to the state's annual $20 billion electricity market in the 1997 session. The state's 83 rural electric cooperatives, serving 3 million Texans, opposed securitization–and they had the votes to kill the bill.

"Apparently there's only a handful of people who really understand how this thing works, and they happen to be bond lawyers," mused Mike Williams, president of Texas Electric Cooperatives. Incidentally, Houston Lighting & Power's $8 billion South Texas Project nuclear plant and Texas Utilities' $11 billion Comanche Peak nuclear plant account for most of the stranded costs in the Lone Star State.

At the federal level, Rep. Schaefer's bill was introduced in a Congress seemingly committed to passing comprehensive federal legislation that would bring retail competition to the electricity industry no later than early 1998. But the bill that seemed a shoo-in at its introduction saw its supporters in both houses of Congress walk away. More and more, the answer that Congress hears is, "Leave electric deregulation and its local complexities to the individual states."

The battle lines have been drawn. Sen. Frank Murkowski, the Alaska Republican who chairs the Senate Energy and Natural Resources Committee, has let it be known that he believes each state ought to decide on electric deregulation within its borders.

This is a pivotal issue–a big money war that will be fought to the finish. You can fully expect this issue to remain controversial for years to come.

LEAVE YOUR WALLET OPEN; THEY'RE STILL NOT THROUGH

As utilities' revenues decrease, their contributions to federal, state, and local tax revenues shrink. If you are really eager to increase your tax bill, agitate for deregulation ASAP–for example, by December 15, 2000, as Rep. Schaefer's bill states. Does this date have some special significance? Will a new comet appear in the heavens, or does the congressman simply want to wrap it all up before Congress's Christmas recess? Why the hurry to ensure a bigger tax dislocation than may be necessary?

The utility shareholder groups have such an obvious stake in maintaining the status quo that it is tempting to dismiss their antideregulatory complaints as overcharged rhetoric, i.e., *self-interest*. Nonetheless, two items bear close attention.

One is the charge that deregulation may jeopardize the value of more than $100 billion in tax-exempt bonds. With numbers of this magnitude, such a charge certainly warrants scrutiny.

Another item for careful consideration is the fact that a huge number of Americans have considerable savings–their retirement savings, in fact–invested in utility stocks. Americans have always looked to the utilities to enhance the quality of their lives and finances through dividends. Ironically, if utility stocks cease paying attractive dividends in order to become growth-competitive, what happens to the quality of life of this vast number for whom utility dividends are the mainstay of their retirement income?

One of the cardinal rules of financial planning is that one should never outlive one's money, so this could be financial euthanasia. If you loved the class-action lawsuits of the oil and gas limited partnerships of the mid-80s (the lawyers loved them), you'll just love this version. Maybe that's what they mean by experienced investors.

Some pundits are dismissing out of hand the potential financial insolvency of these investors as an unfortunate but necessary by-product of the revolution. Customer savings in the tens of billions of dollars will more than outweigh stockholder problems, they say. Ah, yes. Most revolutions rearrange the wealth of the masses; this one will probably be no exception.

Now let's examine a sweeping generality, and again, let's use Congressman Schaefer's bill for illustration.

As he puts it–as almost any politician is going to put it–his bill would "lower the average consumer's bill." But many consumers are already paying lower prices than this "lower average price," and Economics 101 tells us that cheap energy will migrate to higher prices. Many consumers' bills will actually go up. Your bill could be one of them. Is this a case of stranded *benefits?*

In other words, what California's ratepayers (who, remember, now pay an average of 9.4 cents per kWhr) would view as a break is likely to be viewed as exorbitant by Oregonians and Washingtonians, who now reap the benefit of low-cost hydroelectric power–4.8 and 4.2 cents/kWhr, respectively. The reality is that the high energy prices will be lowered significantly, and the low energy prices will rise–perhaps only somewhat, but still rise–depending on the region and the distances involved between the cheap energy and the higher prices.

It's not just hydro, you see. Everybody will want to float with the current that flows from low to high. How about shipping Rocky Mountain natural gas by wire? In other words, generate at the production source or at the wellhead and ship natural gas by wire rather than building pipelines.

When it comes to energy savings, the first question you need to ask yourself is this: Am I a large industrial end-user? This is the category of energy consumer after all, who has been footing the big bills to lobby his state legislators in favor of deregulation. He has been shelling out good money for some time now. Years, in fact. He wants to be rewarded, and he will be.

In an example that is being quoted by consumer groups nationwide, the large industrial end-user in the state of New York is looking at a cost reduction of 25% within five years, thanks to an agreement between the state's Public Service Commission and the state's largest utility, Consolidated Edison. Nothing wrong with that, you say; if industrials' costs decrease that much, the consumer may see lower-priced goods. Right? Very possible. But it's beside the point–the point being that, according to this commission-utility agreement, it looks as if the residential consumer's bill will probably see a reduction of only 3.3%.

Power to the people, right? But which people are you?

CHEF OR ENTREE?

In other words, unbridled, rapid-fire, federally mandated deregulation has some unintended consequences.

The suggestion is being advanced from many different quarters that the headlong rush to achieve a philosophical ideal of pure competition be tempered and paced until all angles of awkward reality are carefully scanned. Reality has an uncomfortable habit of getting in the way of sweeping concepts, and the taxpayer has an uncomfortable habit of not paying attention until it's too late–when unintended consequences bite him bloody.

Okay. So you don't have the income of a neurosurgeon, you've never played the commodities a day in your life, you don't need conversational gambits, you don't want to hear about the revolution's labor pains–you just want to see the kid. You don't care about watts in any size; you just want to sit by your reading lamp.

Here's an illuminating statistic: The power industry is the country's third-largest. It serves a vast, interconnected market, and you're an intrinsic part of it. What does any of this have to do with you? Nothing–unless you pay taxes, have a utility bill, own a motor vehicle, invest in equities or municipal bonds, or contribute to a retirement plan. We are all going to get the bill for the utilities' so-called stranded costs. The size and apportionment of that bill down the road may well depend on how much attention the far-seeing energy user pays to this issue today. So, you may prefer to manage the tab rather than hear a replay of the legendary country and western song, "She got the gold mine, I got the shaft."

•   •   •

The Transcontinental Pipeline brings natural gas from the Gulf of Mexico to New York City. It has done so for more than 50 years. It's a vital link in the national infrastructure, but it's totally out of sight. Out of sight and out of mind.

But consumer complacency is being jolted by the visual impact of more and more power lines as demand increases. Transmission power lines need to be above ground (as opposed to distribution lines, which can be buried) and the NIMBY effect ("not in my back yard") is a pervasive theme in American society. You can ignore all the issues represented by a major natural gas pipeline that snakes under the surface, but how about very visible and humming power lines across your patio? Do you want a voice in that decision?

When it comes to revolutions, you can either help break the eggs, or you can be part of the omelet. Remember that every time we default a decision to somebody else, we're still responsible for the consequences.

Now that you know where to find the revolution and you've been introduced to those likely to be paying for this trip over the barricades and on to the fine mansions built by free choice, it's time to meet a new player–the one who's pulling your choice strings.

Meet Your New Tour Guide

"Power without responsibility—the prerogative of the harlot through the ages."

—Rudyard Kipling

The concept of Hydrocarbon Man was central to the bestseller, *The Prize.*

For most of the 20th century, explains author Daniel Yergin, "If it can be said, in the abstract, that the sun energized the planet, it was oil that now powered its human population, both in its familiar forms as fuel and in the proliferation of new petrochemical products.

Oil emerged triumphant, the undisputed King, a monarch garbed in a dazzling array of plastics. He was generous to his loyal subjects, sharing his wealth to, and even beyond, the point of waste. His reign was a time of confidence, of growth, of expansion, of astonishing economic performance. His largesse transformed his kingdom, ushering in a new drive-in civilization. It was the Age of Hydrocarbon Man."

Just how and why did Hydrocarbon Man become BTU Man? And how does that new creature travel down the BTU value stream?

The BTU stream began as a spring seeping out of rocks; we didn't find oil, it found us. Whale oil was getting increasingly expensive as whales threatened to join the dinosaurs. An alternative fuel was needed to light the industrial revolution. A barrel of crude still has no intrinsic value until it's refined, but in its early days, crude's principal value lay in kerosene as a replacement for the whale oil. When electricity began replacing kerosene as the source of lighting, the value of the barrel of crude was in question. What gave it value again was the evolution of the combustion engine.

Each application led to a dozen others; as applications proliferated, so did the requirement for different energy sources.

In other words, a variety of technological innovations spurred a variety of responses, which in turn created new demand. Remember that demand is the current that always flows to the market. In response to demand, energy sources multiplied, and as they multiplied, many tributaries swelled that initial spring until, with deregulation–the FERC calls it "unbundling"–it became the BTU stream.

The migration path of any commodity is limited only by imagination. If necessity is the mother of invention, then profit is its father. Let's look at electricity.

Its initial use was just for lighting, but now it's the unifying power source at all levels of our society. Because electricity was monopolized almost from its infancy, the only way the nonmonopolist could participate in the value stream was from the outlet outwards–from the point where the consumer took title on the end-user side of the meter. And the nonmonopolist did just that, extending the value stream with the creation of a myriad of products for industrial uses (manufacturing and processing machinery, and fabrication machining, to name only two), agricultural uses, commercial uses, and personal-convenience uses.

The nonmonopolist responded to demand and created demand. Edison didn't envision the hair dryer or electric toothbrush. The marketer did.

BTU Man is really the offspring of Hydrocarbon Man and Electron Man. The latter was monopolized from day one; the former was always largely the by-product of entrepreneurial spirit. There was a vast difference between the two, but they shared a commonality that was greater than their difference. Both streams were product-based and consumer-driven.

BTU Man Disease

Just as all trading is a disease–and if a trader and his employer are lucky, it goes into remission and stays there–so the BTU Man has a basic disease. It's chronic apathy, which realistically equates with a very spoiled consumer.

Hydrocarbon Man had it before him. He created the robber barons by providing the market opportunity in which they thrived; he creates an environment in which all the lower forms of life flourish. He defaults his responsibility to the regulatory bureaucrats, who welcome the job security.

BTU Man drives the value stream. He has the power because he has the dollars. What's more, they're piggyback dollars, both discretionary *and* bare-necessity dollars, both need and want. If you open his wallet, it's hard to tell a necessary from a discretionary dollar. His insatiable need-want for consumer products gives him enormous powers of discretion, but he is largely unaware of what lies at his command. If he is aware, he doesn't do much about it.

If he gets really stirred up, he'll go on boycotts, usually local or at best regional, and always short-lived. In any case, these boycotts are usually misguided, because he is too ignorant of the market to pick the right target. Because market dynamics are always fluid, and the *raison d'être* for the boycott generally appears at the tail end of a pricing cycle, market forces end up snubbing the boycott's noble cause.

To be totally fair to the consumer, he possesses only one mechanism for control. He can ignore the product. A simple weapon, yes, but a witheringly effective one. He who controls demand controls the market. He is in control because he pays for the goods; by withholding the purchase, he exercises control. He governs by pocket veto.

What happens when BTU man decides, in his inchoate, even incoherent, seemingly capricious way, that the pendulum needs correcting?

An example: He swings from giving all power to Detroit to slapping the gasoline-guzzler kings by buying smaller foreign cars. He could go from gasoline to methanol/ethanol and battery-powered cars in a single generation. Yet, BTU Man suffers from the "Vroom Effect." He has to have the muscle car at the same time that he demands a clean environment around him but the demands are made of others, not of himself. (Fig. 3-1)

Fig. 3-1 Will BTU Man ever get over his need for the "Vroom Effect"? The shape and the powerplants have changed, but the spirit exemplified by this late '60s muscle car continues in the current crop of sports cars and sport utility vehicles. (Photo provided by Pontiac Motor Division, General Motors Corporation)

When BTU Man develops the sense that a market segment is getting too powerful–through his inscrutable group-think process that is composed of a mixture of ignorance, indifference, irritation, and paranoia–he slaps socio-political constraints on it. Then he reverses the process. All along, however, he doesn't appreciate the huge power of the demand process he is controlling, or the signals he is sending. He reacts on an individual basis–the making or not making of a personal purchase. In effect, he represents a special-interest group of one, and by doing so he diminishes the overall impact.

The last thing one ever wants is a trader who thinks; a trader is supposed to react. But a consumer who doesn't think through the reason for his decision and then communicates it, is a consumer who doesn't send out signals. This makes it a blind man's bluff game for the marketer.

As long as it is premixed salads, the Game is an expression of the free market at its best. But when the game involves energy, it takes on the dimensions of a huge gamble because of the market size, the inelasticity of demand, and the huge number of dollars involved. It has become even more complicated by the disappearance of the old marketer, and the appearance of a new breed of marketer—one who can best deal with the apathetic/spoiled consumer.

YESTERDAY'S BRAND IDENTITY

Before the revolution, before deregulation, the electricity and natural gas consumer had no choices to make about the basic product, because it was monopolized. He paid the utility for what he used, period.

An impressive variety of electricity- and natural-gas-based products were developed, however, for industrial, commercial, agricultural, business, and residential uses, and marketers promoted these products aggressively on the basis of the product's merits. The consumer and marketer of oil products, especially gasoline, had a great many real-life choices to make and to offer, and again both sides performed on the basis of the product's pros and cons.

The consumer had an identifiable brand to be loyal to; the loyalty came from the belief that one brand of gasoline, for example, made his car perform better than another brand. The marketer knew his product and took pride in its identifiable characteristics, in its superiority or individualism; he mastered the trading regionalisms involved—the so-called *basis*. (See Chapter 7 and Appendix IV.)

With the energy revolution came the free market. The consumers who pushed the revolution forward did so with their minds on cheaper power. If the free market was the way to achieve that, hurrahs for the free market. What they did not agitate for was a slew of products that on closer, time-consuming inspection can be shown to all be the same.

They certainly didn't ask for today's marketer.

Marketer as Tour Guide

Revolutions create at least one good martyr; the energy revolution did not. In its place, this revolution's creation is the Re-Marketer. This gift wrapper has no loyalty to any one brand, not even to his own, and the reason is simple. He really has no product.

It's a long way from New Golden Shell and the proven value of the various performance-enhancing additives. Yesterday's gasoline companies responded to the modern high-compression V-8 engine with higher and higher octane and more and more additives. There was product differentiation. These days the choice among gasoline depends on price and on which side of the highway it's being sold–and mandated oxygen-enhancers do equal damage to all gasoline brands.

In the old brand-identity days, you knew if you got stiffed at the pump. But electricity doesn't make anything go ping if you've been sold the "wrong" kind. You can feel victimized if the house goes dark and the fridge and freezer stop running, the furnace quits, the microwave, TV and VCR are out, towels replace hair dryers, the phone rings but the answering machine doesn't click on, and the cordless and the cellular don't work. Go ahead and feel victimized.

But acknowledge that there's no good electricity, or bad electricity, or a brand that works best with your hair curler. Electricity is there or it is not. A brownout is a brownout for everybody; a power outage is a power outage is a power outage, whether you have a 19-inch TV or a state-of-the-art surround sound system. "Reliability of service" is a great slogan only as long as the current's on. (But how about that great deal on a 35-mm camera stuffed in your electric bill, huh?)

The end result of successful revolutions is more freedom for the revolutionaries, and here the energy revolution is no exception. It gave the new marketer the freedom to sell the illusion of choice.

What is it, exactly, that you are being sold? And how?

The Illusion of Choice

Marketing has taken the form of "Throw more choices at, 'em and see what they'll take." This see-what-sells approach has taken the place of true market research. Why should the Re-Marketer bother with researching the market when he can sell, 'em something right now? After all, he already knows that the American consumer buys emotionally and defends the purchase illogically.

Look at your convenience store—that place where you buy your gasoline, formerly known as the gas station. It's a circus sideshow of choice. How many things can they throw at you to buy before you leave the store—after you've had the privilege of filling your own tank, checking your own oil, and cleaning your own windshield, that is?

The customer, having made the purchase of his choice, must now face the Re-Marketer's Deal of the Day. "For an additional 35 cents, we'll supersize it, dial it for you, or give you one free *plus* the flavor of the day!" The customer is in the escape mode, but for the privilege of using the convenience he must pay his exit fees.

It doesn't stop there, of course. At the end of the month, you get your credit card bill, and that is where the true nature of the marketer-as-tour-guide comes to full flower.

Your credit card bill comes stuffed with so many choices for so many products, that if you bite on even one of them, it's a great success for the marketer. In a masterful trivializing of the revolution, the Re-Marketer has reduced the concept of a free market in energy to pitching 35-mm cameras, restaurant clubs, and card insurance, to name a few.

How much of this stuff do you need? How many different ways can you be pitched with the same stuff that you don't need before you control the avalanche simply by ignoring it? Or, better yet, by leaving the country via the frequent flyer miles free gift you won when you were visiting your local bank or shopping at your local supermarket (which today is often the same thing).

In yet another classic nonenergy example, let's look at the Swiss watchmakers.

They had always assumed that owning a Swiss watch ranked very high on any quality-conscious consumer's list of desires. That was because their products were justifiably prestigious marvels of precise timekeeping. Then the Japanese came along with the Seiko. It was equal in quality to the Rolexes and the Heuers (despite the fact *Seiko* is *Okies* spelled backward) but it was mass-produced, hence, cheaper. And that's what the consumer–except for the status-symbol diehards–really wanted all along, a prestigious marvel of precise time-keeping that happened to be c-h-e-a-p.

Notice that we're still talking product here.

Next, the Japanese jumped on the cutting-edge, electronic-quartz-watch technology bandwagon; they produced a watch finer than the mechanical watch for a mere fraction of the cost. Other countries' industries followed suit; for example, the U.S.-driven Timex is now outmarketing the Seiko.

The Swiss watchmaking industry was hard hit to the point of near extinction, but it fought back and regained market share with a shrewd move, the Swatch watch. In other words, Swiss marketers did their research and correctly read today's younger customer, who does not aspire to the one perfect watch, but rather owns a dozen or more to match different situations, moods, events, outfits, tattoos, whatever.

Still, the whole development was based on *product*.

The United States built the most advanced energy infrastructure in the world under monopoly conditions, in what was called a *natural monopoly*. The revolution has opened and continues to open this infrastructure for everybody to use and choose from. However, all the product choices with which the Re-Marketer is hitting the consumer are merely more ways to get in his wallet through the Illusion of Choice Show, in which the marketer, as the Wizard of Oz, is busy behind his curtain.

Energy is the ultimate marketing game, and it's in the hands of opportunistic Johnnys-come-lately to whom the product is a nonessential–a peripheral consideration.

BEST DEAL ON THE HARBOR TOUR

As was mentioned previously, today's marketer has no loyalty to any one brand, not even his own. This is because his brand is only a means to an end, the vehicle that drives him to market. There is absolutely nothing wrong with the marketer's desire to make money; that's why he's in business. But there is something missing in the consumer-marketer relationship when the marketer becomes nothing more than a "marker-upper"–a time-and space-invading marker-upper. It's a Clark Kent/ Superman identity switch, after all; the Time Bandit is the Re-Marketer *sans* cape.

And his function has come down to this: To find on a daily basis the best prepackaged deals available and then resell them. He is selling all-inclusive vacations; he's turned into a hotel with a good deal on 1,000 tickets for the hydrofoil tour of the harbor. He is flogging the deal of the day that can be repackaged for the most money, for which he can get an attractive rebate.

So all you get is the illusion of choice when all you ever wanted was cheaper juice. The revolution's buzzword has been "unbundling the monopoly's merchant services." Today's marketer is busily bundling. And he bundles away, with the one-stop shop as the ultimate goal, because he doesn't want you capriciously and carefully picking out the itinerary you truly want. You're supposed to buy whatever fits the tour guide's self-interest.

BTU Man should be in open rebellion at this, because energy marketing is in danger of turning into the Book-of-the-Month Club. Is the day coming when the consumer–because of procrastination or other reasons compatible with human nature–does not make the time-sensitive selection and must then accept and pay for the Re-Marketer's product? Is that day already here? How many Book-of-the-Month selections are kept just to avoid a hassle?

Of course, BTU Man possesses the ultimate control by virtue of his checkbook. He has the power to ignore what Time Bandit/Re-Marketer is peddling in his frenzied manner.

What he should *not* ignore is that, through his apathy, he has once again allowed his time and space to be invaded in the bogus cause of consumer choice. BTU Man has already been through deregulation. He's sat through this movie before, but he keeps falling asleep before the ending. When will he learn to sit up, watch the whole thing all the way through the credits, and figure out who was in control? How many admissions is he going to pay? Is he content to just wait, 'til Oscar night to find out who won the award–who won the revolution?

And does the Re-Marketer, he who has no pride of ancestry, also have no hope of posterity? Yes and no. His ranks will thin as the survival of the fittest comes into play.

Funny how evolutions turn out.

SECTION II:
THE SUMMER
TOURIST

THE INVESTOR

"On the frontiers of finance, the last to know is the first to go."
—Anonymous

"The sunshine patriot will, in this crisis, shrink from the service of [his] country."
—Thomas Paine

S o what we have, thanks to a multiplicity of demand, is a mighty BTU stream, made up of multiple energy tributaries. What we also have, thanks to a mighty deregulatory wave, is a stream that everybody can travel on and fish from.

How did this monetization of the molecule–that is, the extraction of its greatest value in its most marketable form in the most advantageous market–come about?

It came about through the commoditization of the energy source. This commoditization came about via the ongoing deregulation of natural gas and electricity–that is, the breakup of government-sanctioned monopolies and the free market that has ensued. In other words, instead of separate and highly regulated energy streams, there is only energy stream, and the freed-up molecule is now the unshackled electron that can make more money for more market players.

Can you imagine what that first soliciting phone call was like?

THE MULLET AND THE RODENT

As we all know every futures market needs liquidity, which is why God put speculators on the face of the earth. And God made commercial hedgers risk-averse, thereby creating an opportunity for speculators to accept this risk in the anticipation of profit.

However, even the most risk-prone speculator requires some comfortable understanding of the market and the particular commodity in order to evaluate his risk-reward opportunity. The two parties go into their ritual dance. The commodity broker calls a high net-worth professional to offer him a trade recommendation. That individual, a.k.a. the speculator, gives the broker a good faith deposit, or initial margin, if he finds the trade idea acceptable.

Before the advent of natural gas futures trading on April 3, 1990, futures trading was fairly simple in that concepts could be visualized. Because all commodity contracts are standardized as to everything except price, most early futures contracts were sized by what could fit on a standard railroad car for transportation to market. Grain, cattle, hogs, lumber, to name a few, were all sized that way–5,000 bushels for grain, 40,000 pounds for cattle, 116,000 board feet for lumber, and so forth. Crude and crude products were equally simple–a 1,000-barrel rail tanker for crude and products, with products being traded in gallons rather than barrels. (For the evolution of the barrel, see Appendix I.)

Then came natural gas and that first phone call. The broker calls his favorite *mullet* (speculator) and advises him to be long (buy) winter gas futures because everyone knows large quantities of natural gas are consumed for heating in the winter and, therefore, the price will escalate substantially. (Unless, of course, there is a mild winter with no major demand on the wellhead or storage supplies, and the Canadians increase exports–but he leaves that out.)

The astute speculator, not about to be hustled by a smooth-talking, commission-motivated broker, begins his series of objections by questioning the vagaries of this new contract. After all, the speculator didn't lose thousands of dollars last year by being stupid!

"What's the contract size?" becomes his intelligent defense to this arcane investment opportunity.

"Oh, yes, the contract size. Well, let's see, it says here on this NYMEX brochure I just received that it's 10,000 MMBTUs."

"What's an *em-em-bee-tee-you?* How big is 10,000 of them?"

"Well, let's see, the contract specs here read that it's the same as 10,000 decatherms."

"10,000 deck*awhats?*"

"Well, it says here that it's also 10 million cubic feet of natural gas."

"Let me get this straight. You want me to speculate on a commodity when I have no idea the size of the contract. I can't see it, can't touch it, can't smell it. I think not. Talk to me about canola futures on the Winnipeg Exchange."

Guess what, speculator? We're now asking you to consider a BTU contract that is 736 megawatts, delivered 2 megawatts an hour, 16 hours a day, for 23 days a month at Palo Verde Switchyard in Arizona or at the California-Oregon Border. You already know what a BTU is, of course. But what's a megawatt?

A *watt* is a unit of power measured in meter-kilogram-seconds. It's equal to one *joule* of work performed per second, or to 1/746 horsepower. An equivalent is the power dissipated in an electrical wire carrying one ampere of current between points at one-volt potential difference. One thousand watts equal one *kilowatt*; one million watts equal a *megawatt*. Twelve hundred residences consume a megawatt, as a rule of thumb, in one hour. Visualize that if you can.

"Wait," you say, "why would the speculator have to know anything about these markets? After all, isn't it the *broker* who has to study these new contracts, analyze them, understand them, and follow them? The neurosurgeon shouldn't have to do any of this." If he does, then what's he got left to talk about? You know—making conversation while he's playing cards at the country club?

It's what the *speculator* has to say about his non-professional activities that makes him a potentially interesting conversational partner. Take away his investment talk, vacation, and golf game and what's left? It's not neural synapses his peers want to hear about, it's the action he's into. Real men may not eat quiche, but they damn sure play commodities. After all, he's a very intelligent man, and like everyone else, he too has his market signals. Why, just this morning he observed the squirrels on the 15th fairway burying acorns for the winter. It's early September; he's never seen this flurry of rodent activity this early in the year. Therefore, he surmises that the animal kingdom is telling him right there at his very own country club that it's going to be an unusually harsh winter. Better be long on January NYMEX gas futures–whatever the hell that is.

His commodity broker confirmed what a brilliant trade idea he had–plus, he said, why not double up to *really* make a killing!

So, the speculator-investor now has new opportunities, lots more choices, and many more products in which to hide his ignorance and confusion. You have to remember that while those squirrels on the 15th fairway may enjoy an impressive track record in natural gas futures, they are somewhat lacking in their equity research.

Is the speculator-investor going to change in order to adapt to the new BTU world? Not likely. He really should start watching the public energy companies as they struggle to reinvent themselves while facing some unpleasant realities and carrying some clumsy baggage from the last energy bust. Unfortunately, he isn't likely to. The speculator-investor has traditionally done a very poor job of carrying out his shareholder responsibility. In fact, he is well known for defaulting his investing responsibility to squirrels. This leads to other rodents infesting the boardrooms. Soon the exterminator walks in.

Remember T. Boone Pickens?

THE SHAREHOLDER'S FRIEND – HE SAID

T. Boone Pickens grew up in the oil patch and was educated as a geologist. He loathed working for the giant oil companies, with their layers upon layers of bureaucratic hierarchies, and soon set out on his own as an independent oil man and cattle feeder. The latter experience gave him an education in futures markets that few of his energy peers possessed, and none appreciated, when crude oil futures began trading in 1983.

Fig. 4-1 Energy industry visionary T. Boone Pickens was interviewed in June 1985, in the offices of PennWell Publishing's Oil & Gas Journal. (Photo by Jim Stilwell)

Early in his career, he began to sense a weakness in the oil business with more vision and clarity than most others did. He realized that the United States was a steadily declining producer with increasingly poor prospects and a continually disappointing and shrinking record of oil and gas discoveries. Pickens was willing to bet that the stock prices of many of the majors did not fairly reflect the liquidation value of their proven oil and gas reserves in the ground.

Here was opportunity waiting to happen. Here was confusion, as well, and as the Latin maxim has it, "In confusion there is profit."

The oilfinder, with his shrewd and analytical mind, was on his way to becoming the corporate raider. Why not drill for oil on Wall Street? The economics of the energy world were now in the balance sheets to be found by the shrewd analyst rather than by the geologist and the drill bit.

In many ways, Pickens was like his peers—oilfield legacy, petroleum geology, early career with the major oil companies—but that's pretty much where the comparisons ended. The former exploration geologist started talking like an analyst. He began preaching that the sum of the parts was often worth more than the whole and pointing to the gap between the stock value and the value of its underlying oil and gas reserves. He became the shareholder advocate. He may have been self-appointed, but shareholders were easily turned into converts to Pickens' crusade. They eagerly followed his banner as he marched into battle to recapture the Holy Grail from the mismanaging corporate infidels. He promised that greater returns would flow from appreciating stock prices and better managed companies.

The first big move by Pickens' Mesa Petroleum, in 1982, was directed toward Cities Service. It was three times the size of Mesa, although its stock was trading at approximately one-third the appraised value of its reserves. By the time the feeding frenzy was over, Occidental had acquired all of Cities Service stock and, although Mesa had not won the bidding war, Pickens' company had made a quick $30 million profit on its acquired shares. The shootout over Gulf, with Mesa losing to Chevron this time, would bring Mesa $500 million—and Pickens a personal bonus of $18.6 million.

The crusade continued as Mesa, Pickens, and the shareholders continued to plunder vulnerable companies. But eventually the value gap closed. Combined with companies' defense mechanisms, such as poison pills, golden parachutes, and higher dividends, this brought the crusaders home from the wars. And Pickens? He's quiet for now, operating a Southern California network of fueling stations for compressed natural gas (CNG) vehicles—until apathy opens another door.

Funny how much candy you can take when the shareholders forget to watch the store, or have it watched only now and then. In the words of Arthur Levitt, chairman of the Securities and Exchange Commission, "I don't care how talented you are, you can't be a good watchdog if you're on patrol only three times a year."

Today, the shareholder has taken his chronic inattention one step further. He has abdicated his responsibility to the corporate analyst. As we'll see in a later chapter, he's having it done. At this point, he doesn't give any indication that he's going to start paying attention. In fact, abdication has worked well in the past; the market has reached record levels—why worry now?

THE KEEPERS OF
THE CASTLE

"The world is disgracefully managed, one hardly knows to whom to complain."

—Ronald Fairbank, *Vainglory*

I n late1982, following a lunar eclipse of the banking industry, the stock market hit an all-time high of 1065.49.

In January 1987, the Dow closed above 2000 for the first time–taking five years to go up just about 1000 points. The next 1000 points took four years. But the following seven years saw an investing frenzy, a 5000-point gain from the beginning of 1991 through the end of 1997.

For years now, we have seen temporary, quick corrections. We have seen industries, such as the biotechnology stocks, go in and out of Wall Street's favor, but we have not seen a sustained bear market.

What effect has this long-playing bull market had on the investing community?

For starters, the number of shares traded has gone up substantially while the number of players has decreased as fund managers have taken over from individual investors. We have become *fund* investors–a defaulting of decision-making on the individual's part. This has worked so far, for a variety of reasons.

So, the market has seen a record high over 9,000. In other words, stock prices have been rising steadily, putting great pressure on corporate earnings to follow proportionately. However, as we know, rising stock prices do not necessarily ensure the growth of corporate earnings. For instance, fund managers may make a significant investment in a given market sector, perceiving it to be "hot." Just as a rising tide lifts all ships, that fund investment will lift the stock price of all companies in that sector, even the stock price of those that are underperforming relative to their peers. This gives the underperformers an undeserved reward–and if you think management does not appreciate the gift, just check the IOQs for recent insider trading. What the rising tide does not do, however, is turn the underperformers into *performers.*

Because of today's increased competition, and customer and analyst demands for corporate earnings–that all-important earnings-per-share (EPS) criterion–to follow the rising stock price, companies must truly perform well relative to their peer group.

That kind of performance has always demanded much more than just good luck, but today a company at any level of the energy industry that outperforms its peers can only do so by having a truly effective risk manager.

A WELL-DESIGNED RISK-MANAGEMENT PROGRAM

Building sustainable competitive advantage that creates and maintains shareholder value is at the core of all the successful business and marketing strategies.

Building such an advantage is especially difficult in the energy field, a field operating in an unregulated free-market economy, where commodity price volatility is the ever-present nemesis. Regardless of its form or function, energy is one of the most volatile commodities–hence, industries–in the world, characterized by global size and complexity, by the world's rising demand for the product, and by the political, environmental, and societal strictures placed on the product.

In the late 1970s (as outlined in Chapter 7), energy futures contracts were introduced to mitigate forward pricing risks. Thus, today's energy participants have an arsenal of financial weapons to manage their risks. The arsenal means that a complex mixture of arcane futures and derivative products can be used in the equally complex and unrestricted global trade. As a result, a well-designed risk-management program is imperative.

The question for today is, how do CEOs and directors recognize a well-designed risk-management program if they don't understand risk management?

Most CEOs and directors in the energy industry are realizing that their survival hinges on their willingness to attack the steep learning curve of the ever-evolving risk-management world. These are multimillion-dollar companies with multimillion-dollar risk. But whose money is it that's truly at risk, anyway? Let's follow the money trail.

On the other side of the table from the energy companies sit the investors. It's their welfare that is at stake. These days, when we say investors, we are really talking about the money managers, the fund companies responsible for managing billions of aggregated trading dollars.

Facing each other across the table, they are actually two fairly equal forces, and each is looking at the same thing, the energy company's grasp and use of the risk-management process and tools. They're focused on the huge black box that sits at the heart of the company, no matter where the company is in the value stream–in producing, transportation, distribution, or any degree of integration thereof.

THE HUGE BLACK BOX

Why is it fair to call a typical energy company's risk-management program a black box? Because its contents and workings are invisible and mysterious, both by nature and by design.

First, let's look at the corporate side. Too often CEOs and directors do not have the knowledge base and tools to adequately assess the company's commodity risk and exposures. They certainly do not know which risk-management instruments and techniques to employ to reach a balance between risk mitigation and risk-taking that is consistent with the company's overall risk tolerance and financial objectives.

This lack of knowledge may be a function of denial, insufficient time and energy, or background or interest. Whatever the cause, the fact remains. As stated earlier, most of them are now aware that they must attain this knowledge base, but, good intentions aside, their attempts are at the initial stage.

THE GENERATIONAL OVERLORDS

There is a powerful subset of CEOs and directors with no intention of ever walking today's risk-management beat.

These executives are in the castle, they enjoy the view, and they perceive the perks and the privileges as their due and reward, not as remuneration for services yet to be rendered. The duty of care is buried in their past. As far as they are concerned, they are grandfathered. They have reached the top of the corporate heap, and they aim to luxuriate in their status and to cement their power by spreading the largesse among like-minded buddies. They also plan to take with them as much of the loot as they can.

For these Generational Overlords, any corporate service rendered is behind them; they do not care if, when they leave, the castle walls are still standing but the castle stands empty. If you believe this to be too harsh an indictment, you haven't been following events reported in the financial as well as the popular media.

This is not just a footnote regarding the recently publicized shenanigans among the captains of industry. The point here is that, with an extremely volatile commodity operating under recent deregulation, the explosive nature of the black box robs the investing public of the luxury of analyzing over time an energy company's steadily declining corporate earnings. When the box blows up, it's past time for useful action by company outsiders.

If the financial landscape ends up littered with gutted castles–bear in mind that the Generational Overlords are mostly attracted to princely manors, not mere one-tower keeps–today's robust and long-lived bull market might reverse into a bear market, or worse yet, reregulation. The Generational Overlords will have made their pile, enjoyed it, and then passed on to that lavishly appointed boardroom in the sky by the time BTU Man discovers the bare stone walls.

ANY TIME BOMBS OR SMOKING GUNS?

Now let's switch to the other side of the table, to those outside the energy company.

These outsiders are the money managers, corporate analysts, and shareholders. The outsiders can adequately determine the energy company's credit-worthiness on a regularly reported basis, but the company's credit *exposure* is another matter. What the outsiders cannot do is look inside the company's risk-management program.

Are there any ticking time bombs, any smoking guns? Is it a coincidence that energy companies have suffered some of the greatest corporate trading losses? Can you blame the outsiders for thinking of the corporate management of commodity risk and exposure as a black box, when the markets have been slapped by the $8-billion-plus losses racked up by the five largest trading disasters just in the mid-'90s?

To take that figure out of Wall Street terms and put it in pari-mutuel terms, it works out to making four *billion* trips to the $2 window at any race track–and losing every time. That's a lot of devotion to the puppies and ponies.

T. Boone Pickens found a situation where companies were undervalued, and he could derive greater value from buying companies and getting control of their reserves than from drilling wells for an equal amount of reserves. What we have today is the reverse.

When a money manager is looking at investing in a company, looking at a balance sheet is like looking at a financial time-freeze frame. It's a look backward. But while it's more profitable to look for what's going on in a company's risk-management program, that activity is hindered by more than the passage of time since the financial snapshot was taken. It's more like trying to peer into the castle's windows, which the keepers have defensively placed behind a moat.

The investing public makes giant bets on how much a stock is really worth without being able to get any kind of a picture of that company's handling of risk and exposure. Analysts give us their criteria for measuring the potential growth of a company, but they have no reliable way to adequately measure a company's potential for dramatic loss through mishandling of risk.

STORMING THE CASTLE

The outsiders' only chance of controlling how a company uses the money invested in it is to make sure that, first, the CEOs and directors care to know what's in the black box, and, second—assuming they care—that they can tell the difference between a bomb and a black safe-deposit box. The only way the outsiders can control the black box is to control those who control it. They must be confident of their risk-management know-how and, to use an old-fashioned word, their character.

Shareholders do not have the legal power to select a company's managers, and most often they have neither the resources nor the expertise to run the companies they invest in. On the other hand, electing the company's *directors* is a shareholder right. And they not only may—they must. The actions of the outsiders exercising this right and duty by acting as watchdogs of their investments has led to what is being called the corporate governance movement.

CORPORATE GOVERNANCE GAINING GROUND

The California Public Employees' Retirement Systems (CalPERS) is the United States' largest public pension fund and the third-largest in the world with more than 1 million members and beneficiaries. It's also one of the corporate governance movement's standard-bearers.

Another is the $100-billion-plus Teachers Insurance and Annuity Association-College Retirement Equities Fund (TIAA-CREF). Still another is the National Association of Corporate Directors. In CalPERS' words, "The corporate governance movement is simply an attempt to revive the rights and duties of ownership."

Three recent studies have provided evidence that good corporate governance pays off. Yale University economist Paul W. MacAvoy, the University of Pennsylvania's Wharton School, and McKinsey & Co. have all shown that well-governed companies not only make more money than the poorly governed, but that investors are likely to give them a higher stock market value.

This ongoing promotion of shareholder activism, which began in the early '90s, is growing quickly; it has now extended to the international markets. The focus of the movement is on the bottom line, its motto is, "Act as an owner," and its main thrust is to establish director-qualification criteria that ensure true independence of directors and of their power to effect corporate change.

The only hope that the outsiders have to evaluate the contents and workings of the black box lies with the individuals who are in control of it—and these are the energy company's directors.

By law, directors have both the authority and the duty to control the company managers. In frequent practice, it is the company managers, a.k.a. the inside directors, who nominate the outside directors into their club. Once nominated and elected, the directors immediately lose their individuality.

RULES FOR WATCHDOGS

What the outsiders need are directors who ally themselves with shareholders, not with management. To bring this about and enable directors to truly govern, a set of reasonable and prudent "best practices" has developed, which the authors endorse (unless or until one or the other is elected to a prestigious board with lots of perks, that is).

- outside directors should be in the majority

- only independent directors should serve on the audit, nominating, and compensation committees

- no former company executives should be on the board

- there should be a mandatory retirement age

- outside directors should meet periodically without the CEO

- a governance committee should be established

- directors should own company stock before being nominated and thereafter all retainers should be in the form of stock

- director pensions should be eliminated

- no director should earn consulting, legal, or other fees from the company

- interlocking directorships should be banned

- measures for frequent self-evaluation of the board's effectiveness should be instituted

This kind of results-driven, independent board is the best tool in the outsiders' search for a view into the black box.

KEEPERS OF THE CASTLE

There is a group whose self-interest dictates that no one–not CEOs, directors, money managers, analysts, or shareholders–should get a working knowledge of the box. This is the group whose members hold the keys to the box.

Just as the monopolists held all the keys to the money machine in the monopoly situation described in earlier chapters, these players are the only ones who have the specialized knowledge required to keep the box running. And they don't want anyone except themselves to know how the box works.

Who are these keepers of the castle? They're the small inner circle of energy and financial players that form the *derivatives market*, a market with balance-sheet requirements that exclude all but an incredibly elite group. Formed during the deregulation of the crude oil and natural gas markets, this group has become the one to hedge the risk of an unregulated power market. Because of the BTU convergence, the players are all the same, the boxes remain interdependent, and the best interest of one most often becomes the best interest of all.

Yes, the incestuous evolution of the energy trading markets has created a tremendous challenge for those legally charged with the responsibility for objective corporate governance over the risk-management processes that is now required not only for the survival, but for the success of the energy trading enterprise of the future.

It is a challenge that the shareholders, the money managers, and the corporate analysts need to meet head-on. And they need to do it sooner rather than later, certainly before today's lustily long-playing bull market reverses into a bear market–and we all agree, don't we, that nothing lasts forever?

Section III:
The Journey

THE GREENING OF THE AGENCIES

"Power is nothing without control."
—Pirelli tire advertisement

J ust when did regulatory agencies turn ugly?

Sometime in the 1980s, regulation became downright un-American—ironically, some 100 years after its birth as a typically American institution. It was in 1897 that the Interstate Commerce Commission was established, with the mandate to regulate railroad issues. It was the first of many regulatory agencies to come.

Existing governmental bodies, from federal departments to state legislatures, couldn't deal on a continuous or apolitical basis with the highly technical complexities and/or politically charged issues arising from the country's industrial explosion. Regulatory agencies were specifically created to take over the task.

The agencies went about their work, which was to foster the birth and development of a massive infrastructure of necessary societal services, funded predominantly by investors sheltered under monopolistic regulatory protection.

The infrastructure developed in an America of strong, tightly knit geographic communities, a country that remained vastly rural despite the frenetic pace of industrial growth fueled by dizzying technological invention. But today's America is part of a global marketplace that puts enormous competitive pressure on its service sectors. Plus, today's society is one of instantaneous information and of niche markets. It's a totally different world from even a quarter-century ago.

And the cry is heard, "Let's scrap this feeble leftover of an America that's dead and buried!" But before the profit-driven, the predators, and the historically unaware get to preside over the regulatory agencies' last rites, let's look back at some creative experimental surgery that had huge unintended consequences.

The public should have demanded second opinions.

ROUTE 66: THE ROAD THAT BUILT AMERICA

This was the first highway to link the Midwest with the West Coast. Built in 1926, the 2,400-mile route spanned eight states and three time zones and quickly became a major route of commerce. Its narrow two-lane pavement spawned diners, gas stations, motor courts, and billboards–later called fast-food restaurants, service stations, motels, and mass media–and, eventually, waves of nostalgia.

Route 66 also spawned the Interstate Highway System, which took off in the 1950s as an ongoing government program to build a 42,000-mile national network of multiple-lane, dual expressways connecting 48 states and 90% of all cities with a base population of 50,000. This system was intended to promote interstate commerce and national security by making it possible to drive from coast to coast without stopping for a traffic light. And it did.

The system also made it possible for the traveler to bypass the business districts of smaller population centers on the system. These towns countered with off-ramps, but those areas immediately off the ramp quickly became congested with nationally franchised fast foods, and service station and motel chains. The free-market economy thrived, and many main streets and towns slowly dried up along with the local businesses.

The local utility is facing the same scenario, as power marketers will be able to bypass it by directly offering its customers competitive products.

DON'T BANK ON REGULATION

Just like electric utilities, banks have experienced the advantages and disadvantages of the protection provided by the regulatory process. Traditionally, bank regulators erected barriers to those wishing to enter banking and closely monitored the loans that could be made. As a result, banks lost a great deal of their market share and much of their core business to new, non-industry competitors that were not under the same regulatory constraints. As the '70s came to a close, banks tried to fight back by taking increasingly greater risks in order to achieve greater returns. Unfortunately, this daring strategy didn't work and led to the disastrous bank failures of the '80s, culminating in even more stringent regulatory oversight.

The '90s found the banks fighting back again, but this time through the creation of an over-the-counter, derivative-product market that would compete successfully with highly regulated stock and commodity exchange-traded instruments. Thus, they began competing with many of the same industries that had invaded them.

A review of the banking industry tells us that market forces will find a way to circumvent regulatory restraints that impede the natural evolution of the marketplace, and that industries under attack cannot wait for leadership or timely protection from lawmakers or regulators. It also tells us that competition is not static. Today's winners may be tomorrow's losers.

HIGH-TECH TELECOMMUNICATIONS

The U.S. telecommunications industry evolved from the fully integrated Bell System as it fell victim to regulatory and judicial interventions. The interveners initially inhibited competition, only to reverse course and promote it. The intense competition created by this on-again, off-again regulation has greatly affected every level of consumer in this country. At the same time, the telecommunications industry has been greatly affected by technology, with advancements and breakthroughs that have vastly altered the economics of communication services.

Technology should be viewed as an opportunity, not as a cost item; new products and services are natural by-products of change. The lesson for today's energy utilities is that they cannot continue to rely on regulatory protection and traditional revenue vehicles.

Possibly the most important lesson to be derived from the telecommunications experience, however, is that consolidation inevitably brought on by runaway competition may result in too few competitors. Today we are seeing higher prices than under Ma Bell's monopoly. We're also seeing a few vast power bases asking the courts for protection against uppity small businesses invading their sacred turf. These developing turf wars may once again create regulatory intervention.

Remember, when you open the clubhouse doors to everybody who wants in, you never know who's going to show up and you never know their true handicaps; plus, because there are just so many golfers one set of greens can support, they start fighting for tee times. As a result, membership will dwindle until the club returns to exclusivity–unregulated exclusivity at that.

In other words, deregulation may well end up creating behemoths that act as an oligopoly, and consumers end up losing. Again.

Oops. The Energy Revolution just electrocuted itself.

TRUCKS AND PLANES

Two additional casebook studies in deregulation are the trucking and airline industries, both of which learned how to lose colossal sums of money in the fare wars that followed deregulation.

Just like the utilities, both industries used to rely on the regulators to allow them to make rate increases to pass price volatility on to the consumer. Without the shelter of the regulatory umbrella, they were forced to learn that unhedged and volatile fuel prices can sharply escalate operating costs, adversely affecting earnings per share, sometimes to the point of no return. Deregulated, unprotected markets proved to be a steep learning curve, one that brought many in the transportation industry to a halt.

The industry's consumers quickly learned that without the cost-protective benefits of regulation, the cost of their goods and services would rise. The larger companies flooded competitive routes with low to bargain-basement fares, only to raise prices again after driving the smaller companies off the route and out of business. Some consumers at inconvenient locations off main routes learned that whole services could disappear. In fact, whole fleets and airlines *did* disappear. Quick now, business traveler: How many airlines served you in 1978, when airlines were deregulated? How about 10 years ago? And how many choices do you have today?

It bears repeating: As deregulation continues, inevitable consolidation may once again create regulatory intervention. The rhetoric-rich turf war between United Airlines and Frontier Airlines is illustrative (and other players at other airports can be substituted at will). Frontier's charges revolve around an alleged 15-year pattern of predatory pricing on the part of United, the world's largest airline. This below-cost pricing, says Frontier, violates the spirit of the deregulatory federal legislation.

In its formal complaint to the U.S. Department of Justice, Frontier pointed to United's 66% market share and its "predatory, anti-competitive and monopolistic practices" at Denver International Airport (DIA), one of the two domestic airports United calls its superhubs and Frontier's home hub. Travelers using DIA pay the highest unrestricted airfares in the country, Frontier charged.

United filed its own complaint with the U.S. Department of Transportation charging Frontier with seeking preferential treatment. "In essence," said United President and Chief Operating Officer John Edwardson, "Frontier's real complaint is that United is competing with it. Frontier would rather cooperate than compete."

The media has covered the whole thing in David-and-Goliath terms and that's apt. (Of course, advertising firms have been the major beneficiaries.) But this outbreak is only a symptom of the real disease. The important question for the diagnostician to ask is, what best serves the interests of the flying public, not just today, but in the future as well?

Since the advent of competition, more than 60 airlines have closed their doors and others are being inevitably squeezed out of existence. Perhaps in some industries the public's interest is best served by regulation after all–the kind of regulation that gives the flying public a fighting change when the friendly skies are not so friendly.

THE SACRED INDUSTRY

Medicine was the quiet profession. It spelled dignity–a white, starched, sterile image. The medical field had no formal regulatory oversight; it required none. Competition was simply not an issue.

However, by the early '80s, Americans had become very concerned about rising healthcare costs and equally fearful of a socialized-medicine solution. The cure-all: Competition. Medicine became "the healthcare industry"–one like any other, with mergers and acquisitions, intensive advertising, and aggressive marketing.

PPOs, HMOs, and others have replaced the health-indemnity contract that created this country's modern healthcare system. Consumers now have their choice of plans, cost structures, medical personnel, and facilities, while healthcare providers monitor cost, recommendations, tests, second opinions, and all facets of administration and marketing.

Thus, a whole new administrative layer has been interjected. This new business remedy makes huge profits through the brokering of access to medical services–offering benefits packages to companies and then cutting the costs of these benefits via mass contracting with healthcare organizations. So, in an effort to control costs, we've created the potential for enormous gains for the managed-care companies that intervene between patient and provider.

The once quiet, dignified profession is now an advertising game. What competition has brought is a landscape wherein the newly created administrative layer is the real winner. Even though the medical profession was not a monopoly, it once held the key to an enormous money machine. Consumers, by demanding choice, value, and quality at low cost in a free, unsocialized market, allowed the marketers access to the money machine.

All in the sacred name of competition.

Toss the Whole Thing?

None of what has been written above is meant as an attack on deregulation or a defense of regulatory agencies. It's meant as a question of what constitutes prudent and reasonable balance. The agencies were conceived more than a century ago to handle a continent's coming of industrial age. They have gotten gray and stodgy. At best, they are bureaucratically unresponsive to urgently needed change and innovation; at worst, they exercise ineffective control over the utilities and service companies they allegedly regulate. But was it the regulatory *concept* that failed? Or is the agencies' ineffectiveness more a function of antiquated structure and retrovision?

It's human nature to ignore and/or minimize the successes of previous generations by looking at them through today's eyes. Regulatory bodies have had two basic mandates, to protect utility customers from poor service and unfair charges resulting from a misuse of the monopoly status of the utilities and to assure fair treatment for the utility investors. Largely, they succeeded. Would any of this country's solid infrastructures have been built without a regulatory guaranteed rate of return?

Hasn't the economic performance of many utilities been impressive, accounting for a significant percentage of the nation's capital investment while providing a wide variety and high quality of services?

It has been obvious for a long while that today's issues need different handling than yesterday's regulatory structure can provide. But is it regulation that's outmoded or even evil? Do we want the nation's infrastructures operating without any sort of control?

If what BTU Man wants is totally unbridled competition, he needs to be prepared for the consequences, intended or otherwise.

HEALTHY UNIT OR CARCASS?

So, before staking out the local utility for animals of prey to pick clean, let us remember that a weakened animal can't perform useful functions, a starving horse can't carry you for long.

Utilities, you see, are not being voted out. Under California's AB 1890, under other states' deregulatory structures, and under legislation debated elsewhere, it is the *generation* of electricity that becomes a commodity to be bought and sold in the marketplace like any other. For the foreseeable future, transmission and distribution—the so-called natural monopolies—continue to be regulated by the state and conducted by the utilities.

The reconfigured utility will be different from what we grew up with. Unlike other big businesses—baseball teams, radio stations—the utility was never dashing. It was the rock-solid asexual caretaker, like moms, schoolteachers, and librarians. There's never been a TV series, *As Your Utility Turns.*

A majority of Americans grew up being told, "If you smell gas, run to your neighbor and call your utility. You want an investment that's unspectacular but safe as mother's milk, sock your money into Your Utility. You want job security, work for Your Utility."

We've come almost 180 degrees away from that when today's adherents of a totally competitive market can't wait to see the regulatory framework dismantled. But we ought to keep some considerations uppermost in our minds.

Let's listen to Norman Augustine, the CEO who took then-Martin Marietta from a downward plunge to today's Lockheed Martin success: "The penalty one pays for this [successful survival] is fewer competitors. But as long as there are at least two strong competitors, in my experience that's adequate. If you fall below two, there would be reason for grave concern."

That sound you heard was President Teddy Roosevelt, the great antitrust fighter, turning over in his grave. "Reason for grave concern?" Falling below two gives one. One means monopoly. Something just happened to the lower prices resulting from an open-access market. Do we want an unregulated monopoly in the defense-aerospace industry?

Do we want an unregulated monopoly in *any* industry?

Deregulation must be accompanied by an overseeing agency committed to more vigilance, not less, regarding potential antitrust activities.

In dealing with energy, we are dealing with the country's finite resource base, with its electric grid, its public safety, public health, public commitment. We are dealing with critical factors such as convenience and reliability of service. BTU Man can do without the convenience of his electric toothbrush, but to the hospital's emergency room, reliability of service is more than a convenience.

Let's ask ourselves some questions. What happens when an unsupervised utility, feeling harassed by competition, puts short-term profits ahead of improvements or even ordinary maintenance? *At best*, an outage–but how about the entirely possible at-worst scenarios? What happens with the reality of consumers unable to pay for heat and light? Do we want to scrap public oversight and let the very poor and their children, the aged and the infirm, freeze to death in the dark?

Then there's the whole environmental question. For a historical perspective on what happens when human nature meets unbridled competition, study the oilfield excesses detailed in Chapter 8. Environmental organizations such as the Natural Resources Defense Council, the Solar Energy Industries Association, and the American Wind Energy Association fear that open, unsupervised competition will do serious harm to incentives for conservation of finite resources and even kill off renewable energy industries. They say this, even though a limited market for "green power" (that is, environment-friendly energy, such as solar and wind power) will continue to be offered to those willing and able to pay for it.

It is to be hoped, of course, that those who pay premium prices for green power will be able to tell a green electron when it comes in over the wire.

DENIAL, ACCEPTANCE, GROWTH?

There are 3,050 electric utilities in this country; of these, 150–the members of the trade association called the Edison Electric Institute–generate about 75% of the country's electricity and serve some 75% of its electric consumers. The remaining 2,900 are much smaller than the EEI elite is; some are very small indeed.

The deregulation of an industry removes layers of regulatory protection and, thereby, increases competitive pressures. Typically the result is downsizing, consolidations, spin-offs, hostile takeovers, and a number of other spirited corporate changes. The competitive pressures just described are often very difficult to ignore. Oddly enough, many utilities try. Utilities that try to ignore the changes and opportunities of deregulation are like those absent-minded souls who forget to set their clocks forward in the spring at Daylight Savings Time, so they always have one hour less than they think and they sleep through that all-too-important opportunity.

A lot of utilities started out in total denial. They've gotten better at facing the oncoming unpleasantness, but they still have a way to go.

In addition to struggling with denial, increasing competition, decreasing margins, and the need to reinvent its corporate structure, today's utility faces two major challenges. The first is that electricity, as you've learned by now, is going to be the most volatile energy market on the continent, combining a fuel mix of gas, oil, coal, and hydro. It includes staggering pricing complexity and a market that goes seven days a week and features peak and off-peak periods.

Utilities will find futures, options, and derivative products increasingly necessary for hedging risks not previously faced in regulated markets, but new business practices and competition will make for a very steep and highly exposed learning curve. Many of the BTU merchants busily converting hydrocarbon molecules to electrons will have trading skills in natural gas; out of the top five nonutility power marketers, three are also among the top five gas marketers. Others will have skills in financial products, and they will be eager to capitalize on the arbitrage opportunities in the hydrocarbon-electricity spreads. (The BTU merchants and their tools are discussed in the next chapter.)

The other major challenge faced by utilities is the urgent need to augment traditional profit centers. The defense-aerospace industry offers an encouraging example to follow.

With the race to the moon won, the U.S. drifted back into complacency. First the space program's costs, then its very existence came under attack. With the end of the Cold War came a near-fatal tailspin. But the industry, in the midst of the loss of some 50% of its market and more than 1.5 million of its highly educated specialists, moved into the commercial marketplace. Lockheed Martin chairman Augustine has outlined his company's transition.

"We're committed to defense, but our principal area of growth over time will be in the commercial arena…into commercial products that very closely relate to our core skills…new product lines that are high-tech and systems-oriented, that involve large customers and growth markets. Today in our industry we've been able to generate substantial savings for our customers."

NEW ROLES FOR BOTH

What will help the utility survive as a transformed, healthy unit? Who can help it in its new role? The regulatory agency–in *its* new role.

Part of the regulator's duty will be to support the utility in finding and mastering the risk-management tools and concepts basic to survival and growth, while the largest commodity market in North America deregulates all around that utility's walls.

Today's regulator can fill a vital role in assisting the utility in following the successful path of the defense-aerospace industry. It can help develop the incentives and support necessary for its progress into new markets. And it can keep it from repeating the defense-aerospace industry's disastrous record of layoffs (many of which continue to be litigated, over age-discrimination and other issues).

Today's regulatory agencies must examine those strategies that deal with the inevitable consolidation and reinstitutionalization of most basic utility service sectors. Whatever we choose to call this new order–deregulation, reregulation, or controlled competition–regulatory agencies still must answer their basic 100-year-old, public-oversight mandate: Assure the consumer of a reliable and affordable BTU source, assure the investor of a reliable and profitable investment, and protect the resource and society from the ever-circling predator.

THE MATURING OF THE BTU MERCHANT

"What we anticipate seldom occurs; what we least expect generally happens."

—Henrietta Temple

"Future shock is the dizzying disorientation brought on by the premature arrival of the future."

—Alvin Toffler

Did you know that there was an active rice futures market traded along the Yellow River in China more than 3,000 years ago?

Did you know that Dutch whalers in the sixteenth century entered into forward sales contracts for their whale oil before sailing? That a tulip futures contract was traded in Holland in the 1700s?

To fully understand today's accelerating energy revolution, we must understand that commercial forward sales contracts and futures markets have very long taproots and have become very interdependent. The result is a strong family likeness between the BTU merchant of today and the grain merchant of 150 years ago.

Futures trading within the United States appears to have begun before the railroad days of the 1850s with the Midwest grain merchants. They bought wheat from outlying territories but were not sure when they would obtain delivery or what their quantity would be. Under these conditions, the introduction of to-arrive contracts enabled the sellers to get a better price for their grain, and the buyers to avoid serious price risk.

Any trader–BTU, grain or whatever–needs to have a forum, an exchange. Exchanges are established as a centralized cash market in response to the needs of buyers and sellers of commodities for a central marketplace that draws large numbers of prospective buyers and sellers while providing rules for ethical trading practices and reliable, uniform standards of weights and measurements. The oldest existing U.S. commodity futures exchange is the Chicago Board of Trade (CBOT), founded in 1848. Shortly thereafter came the Chicago Mercantile Exchange (CME) and the Kansas City Board of Trade (KCBT). The latter is now the only grain-trading exchange to join the BTU merchants with its Western Natural Gas Futures and Options Exchange.

As was hoped, a centralized marketplace increased marketing efficiency by increasing the competition between buyers and sellers. However, it did not solve the problems inherent in the production and marketing of commodities, that is, the alternating periods of supply and demand that could lead to extreme price fluctuations and, hence, to price-risk exposure.

Grain producers, marketers, and end-users had a basic problem. They had a one- to three-month harvest period with which to supply a market throughout a twelve-month consumption year. Putting the grain in storage and pulling it out without a futures market offers no price protection. The grain exchanges provided the opportunity to take the peaks and valleys out of their purchases and sales. How? By allowing each to price independently of the other.

The trader doesn't always have the buyer and the seller matched–mirrored, as he says–so he needs a forward market until he can mirror his buy/sell portfolio. Remember that futures markets exist only in relation to cash markets; these are the underlying primary markets in which actual physical commodities are bought and sold. Price volatility is inherent in all commodities, and that volatility becomes a great source of financial risk for all of those who produce, market, process, or consume these commodities or the products derived from them.

Shortly after the founding of the CBOT, grain brokers began trading in *cash-forward contracts* as a means of assuring buyers a source of supply, and sellers the opportunity to sell forward throughout the year. This simple process allowed buyers and sellers to agree upon a predetermined amount of grain to be delivered at an agreed-upon future date. It allowed producers to sell manageable amounts of grain to market numerous times throughout the year. Forward contracting also allowed purchasers to meet their continuous merchandising and processing needs for the entire year. In many cases, cash forward contracts were left unspecified until the time of actual delivery.

As one can well imagine, supply and demand conditions ensuing between the time of contracting and delivery kicked up many disputes in contract value. As the use of cash-forward contracting grew in popularity, the *futures contract* evolved as we know it today. The difference between the two is that futures contracts are specified as to the price at the time the contract is made, as well as quantity, quality, delivery location, and time of delivery.

The evolution of futures contracts introduced the concept of both buyers and sellers posting *margin* (good-faith deposits) with a third party to ensure contract performance.

PRESENT-DAY FINANCIAL MARKETS

Curiously enough, the evolution of grain markets provides a great deal of insight into today's BTU world.

As they evolved, grain markets began laying the foundation of present-day financial markets. As global markets emerged and found new heights of volatility in deregulated economies, futures became increasingly necessary for precious metals, currencies, interest rates, and the world of energy.

Like most other North American exchanges, the New York Mercantile Exchange (NYMEX) evolved out of prosaic country beginnings. It was originally founded to trade dairy products in 1872, the same year that John D. Rockefeller launched "Our Plan" at Standard Oil to take over the American oil industry and eliminate competition. It was named the Butter and Cheese Exchange; then Egg was added. But the name soon changed to the New York

Mercantile Exchange as potatoes, onions, apples, plywood, and platinum joined the dairy mainstays; in fact, potatoes became the principal NYMEX commodity.

In the late 1970s, however, declining market conditions resulted in the termination of potato trading. Threatened with possible extinction, the exchange introduced the No. 2 Heating Oil Contract in 1978. It worked.

Then the industry's guiding dinosaur angel intervened and decided that OPEC had been dictating global prices long enough. The world was ready for a new global pricing mechanism and risk-management tool–and the NYMEX would have its chance by providing the trading-floor anonymity that the merchants were looking for.

The rest is a part of BTU history–past, present, and future.

BEGINNINGS OF BTU WORLD

Gasoline futures, in 1981; crude oil futures, in 1983; natural gas futures, in 1990; and electricity futures, in 1996 duplicated the success of the Heating Oil Contract. Also introduced were the options on futures contracts associated with each energy contract. The BTU world had begun.

First, it was Standard Oil that established the price of crude oil; the Texas Railroad Commission followed it in the United States as did the majors overseas. Then came OPEC's turn. Now comes the age of instantaneous price transparency and communication established by open outcry in the futures exchanges' trading pits. Successes and failures are now determined at the speed of light. Traders no longer have the luxury of thinking through a problem. Instantaneous communication requires instantaneous decision.

How does that unfunny joke go? A lawyer's mistakes are in jail; a doctor's mistakes are in the graveyard; but a trader's mistakes are there for the world to see.

Today's commercial hedgers, just like their grain merchant predecessors, must weigh the traditional cash-purchase and sales alternative against physical forward contracts (both spot and term) and listed exchange contracts (both futures and options). But the BTU hedger now has an exhaustive array of financial tools available with over-the-counter (OTC) instruments. (An OTC transaction takes place outside a listed exchange; it's a principal-to-principal transaction that is unregulated by any listed exchange or governmental agency, with each party relying solely upon the other's financial integrity and credit worthiness.)

Easy decisions–not that they were ever that easy–are a thing of the past. Using these numerous pricing alternatives to the BTU merchant's most favorable advantage requires a thorough understanding of physical market fundamentals and sophisticated marketing skills in price risk-management tools. Because these are OTC tools, and therefore unregulated, none of them come with warning labels or instructions. And paradoxically, the more tools the BTU merchant invents to become risk-averse, the greater the risk potential he actually creates.

THE ILLUSION OF CONTROLS

Advances in knowledge mean opportunity. However, windows of opportunity in a technological world are open only so long.

"I don't worry about my competition passing me," says James E. Rogers, vice chairman and CEO of Cinergy Corporation. "I worry about technology passing me."

And as tomorrow becomes today too quickly, as your competition easily performs reverse engineering on your product (which is mostly non-proprietary), technology becomes a narcotic.

It is precisely this rapid-fire telecommunications capability and this proliferation of tools and financial instruments that make controls so vital and, at the same time, almost illusory. The greater the number of choices to be made at faster and faster speeds, the harder it is to exert control, especially over the young traders, whose inexperience is surpassed only by their youthful arrogance and their technological, computer-age whiz-kid skills. The older traders, who are expected to serve as mentors and supervisors, possess all kinds of experience; they may even have marketing skills (in which most floor traders do not excel), and they may even listen to what the world outside the pit floor is saying. But what they do not possess is the fluency of the younger traders with today's technological advances. Also, they generally lack the people skills to recognize the truly dangerous specimens among the younger traders. That may be the most glaring pitfall of all when it comes to controls in the world of the BTU trader.

Remember Nick Leeson? He was the 28-year-old whose totally unsupervised activities single-handedly brought down prestigious Barings Bank of London (an institution whose experience, incidentally, included financing the Louisiana Purchase in 1803). Why was he so spectacularly unsupervised? Because management tends to not fix what seems to be working. If the trader appears successful, management ignores dangerous symptoms.

You think small children are hungry for heroes? Well, they pale in comparison with corporations, who are *starving* for heroes. When they think they've found one, they give him free rein. If he makes a noticeably bad trade (one even senior management recognizes), he might get criticized, but if he doesn't make a trade, he gets fired. Management expects action.

When a newcomer brings totally innovative ideas into a corporation, especially from other industries, top management tends to dismiss any criticism by longtime staffers as proof of jealousy or fuddy-duddy ways, The newcomer is not only inadequately supervised, he is left to act at will. Unfortunately, the rogue trader nearly always enjoys the protection of an older and well-established executive who admires some trait the trader possesses, and that he, the big gun, lacks.

The two individuals have one common trait, however—uncontrollable ambition.

THE FORECASTING FALLACY

What technology does superbly well is to amplify the weaknesses of human nature, and as we know (to our sorrow) nobody ever went broke underestimating those. The more aggressively competitive the trader, the more he gets put on the trading desk.

When you put a forecast in front of that kind of temperament, you don't have to say, "We've gotta beat this!" That message is implied.

In the boardrooms, the corporate dictum is, "We have to meet these projections!" To even the least aggressive corporate survivalist, this translates into, "Beat—not meet."

To the pit-bull trader, it screams, "Hit a homerun!"

As Yogi Berra said, "I always knew the record would stand…until it got broken."

Marksmen need a bull's-eye to shoot at. Traders need a forecast to beat.

A typical dictionary definition of forecasting is, "Calculating or predicting some future event or condition usually as a result of rational study and analysis of available pertinent data."

In any industry, forecasting is a widely accepted tool the corporation uses to meet its objectives. However, while forecasting is a necessary tool, it can become a snare and a delusion if it is indiscriminately used and slavishly followed. For example, the banking debacles of the 1980s were caused by failed forecasts and not by the oil and gas industry's flawed exploration and production (E&P) practices.

On the utility side, what happens when you have a failed forecast? The large end-user gets to settle up on the back nine; the residential customer gets to pay for the miscalculation.

There are myriad examples of forecasts that over-relied on technological breakthroughs and failed because of the hugely unintended consequences that tend to erupt in the wake of these breakthroughs.

As Yogi liked to point out to sportswriters after he had become a coach, "Forecasting is very difficult, especially when it concerns the future."

If forecasting is used as a tool to help focus management's thinking, it generally works. It's when forecasting is used as a tool of corporate ego that trouble comes. When a device to assist in planning gets all wrapped up with the corporate image, what happens when the forecast is wrong? Do we raise the bridge or lower the river? We just change the forecast, don't we? But that has put the trader in a no-win situation, because traders must always beat a competitor's forecast, even if they know it's ridiculous. That's their job. They trade for a profit.

The risk manager, who is over the traders, is the reactionary trader, if you will. He needs to keep everything in balance, to mitigate or neutralize risk in any given situation. Unfortunately, most risk managers are really nothing more than traders with seniority whose trader's disease is in remission. If forecasting is an inexact science–and it certainly is, as you can't control what you can't expect–will better risk managers mean better forecasting?

The Penn Square Bank failure of 1982 came before the futures and options contracts in crude oil and natural gas. Had it been possible to forward-sell the forecast's inflated yield curve promulgated by the Carter Administration–in other words, to use the derivative tools the BTU trader now has at his disposal–the forecast would have been validated.

Had the Japanese, for instance, with their known yen for a good deal, purchased the Penn Square derivatives, Penn Square Bank would have flourished, and Mitsubishi rather than Continental Illinois might have been the one sucking the regulator's swamp water. It would have been a truly unintended consequence–and an ironic payback for our having subsidized for so long Japan's cheap energy that fueled that country's industrial engine.

Let's look at yet another instance of totally unintended consequences–only this one has a good ending. Let's call this one, *The Bad, the Ugly, and the Good.*

When banking regulators in 1982 slammed Penn Square Bank to the ground so fast and hard, they obviously had not considered the house-of-cards effect. Hundreds of banks failed within one year. Penn Square was the Bad; the regulators were the Ugly.

In 1994, a flawed forecast led to a misinterpretation of the yield curve, causing Metallgesellschaft of Germany to mismatch a number of long-dated swaps against an equal number of futures contracts stacked in the front months and continuously rolled forward. The result was a lag in cash-flow payments, and another house-of-cards collapse was in the making. But (here comes the Good!) a group of international banks–and not regulators–stepped in with a sizable cash infusion to bridge the mismatched lag in cash flows.

The industry had learned a lesson from the Penn Square debacle. The command must be calm and dispassionate, not panicked and self-important. It must come from seasoned veterans, not bureaucrats with an ax to grind. The command is ready, aim, fire. It's not ready, fire, aim.

THE BASIS

Two of the most important physical market fundamentals to understand—and two of the least understood—are the *physical-futures price relationship* and the *arbitrage opportunities* created by physical-futures contract deliveries.

When trading any commodity that is listed on a futures exchange, it is critical to understand the ever-changing relationship between the physical commodity and the exchange futures price. This relationship is known as *the basis* or *basis differential*. The only risk the commercial hedger has is in basis risk; therefore, all energy hedgers become traders of the basis. And basis becomes the economics of where and when. (For an explanation of basis, see Appendix IV.)

In natural gas trading, the early energy merchants came into prominence because of their knowledge of regulatory issues as deregulation emerged. Post-1978 natural gas marketers were typically more familiar with the bureaucratic hierarchies than with the actual transportation and marketing of the molecules. Their role was more that of a filing clerk or intermediary than of a trader.

As the world of deregulation matured, marketers became more motivated by the arbitrage opportunities presented by *location disparities* than those of merely nominating the gas with the required regulatory filings for a mark-up paid by the producer or end user of 1-cent-per-Mcf (1,000 cubic feet—see Appendix II).

What is different for the BTU merchant?

With the oncoming deregulation of electricity, the trader will deal with an energy source that, unlike hydrocarbons, cannot be stored. He will have gone from playing the dynamics of the storage game to just-in-time deliveries. But this is more of a difference on the surface than in reality, for two reasons.

• One, there's another name for storage in the electric world, and it's

 peak capacity.

- Two, modern plants have the capability of generating electricity extremely quickly.

This brings us to an interesting location disadvantage, different yet similar to the arbitrage opportunities available in today's basis.

This is *heat rate*–that is, the measure of efficiency in converting input fuel to electricity. Heat rate is expressed as the number of BTUs of fuel (i.e., natural gas) per kilowatt-hour (or BTU/kWhr). Heat rates for power plants depend on the individual plant design, its operating conditions, and its level of electric power output. The lower the heat rates, the more efficient the plant. It follows that plants with the ability to burn low-cost, environmentally clean natural gas would probably have an economic advantage over older plants that burn a higher-cost, higher-sulfur fuel, such as No. 6 Heating Oil.

What it all boils down to for the BTU merchant is this: He has a product. Where is it worth the most money and in what form? Is a molecule worth more than an electron, and if so, where? This is a concept in the commodity world known as *tolling*. In other words, is the sum of the parts worth more than the whole?

Crude oil really has no value until it is refined, so it's the value of the refined products (gasoline, heating oil, jet A, naphtha, etc.) that determines the value of the unrefined barrel of crude. In trading jargon, this is referred to as the *crack spread*.

In futures trading, a spread is the simultaneous purchase of one futures contract and the sale of a different futures contract. An example of a 3-2-1 *summer crack* would be buying 3 NYMEX June crude oil futures contracts and simultaneously selling 2 NYMEX July unleaded gasoline futures contracts and selling 1 NYMEX July No.2 heating oil contract. This 3-2-1 *crack spread* defends the refiner's margin by neutralizing the threat of increasing crude oil cost and declining refined product prices. The spread of the future–the *spark spread*– is the one to watch, because it features natural gas versus electricity.

Fittingly, bootleggers were the first energy tollers and probably the first to come upon the crack spread, because they were the first to crack a barrel. When crude oil was discovered in Pennsylvania, the first refining efforts to obtain the much-needed kerosene came from the bootleggers, the only ones with the knowledge to toll an ear of corn into moonshine. They literally distilled those early barrels of crude into usable products in their moonshine stills.

Isn't it a good thing that crude was discovered in Pennsylvania and not the Napa Valley?

TRADING BY NECESSITY

Ken Nichols of Nichols Consulting offers an interesting comparison between British Petroleum (BP) and today's sale of power plants by the major utilities.

BP became a global trader of crude oil through sheer necessity. In 1982 it lost 40% of its crude supply when Iran, Nigeria, Kuwait, Iraq, and Libya nationalized (read, seized) it. Without this supply, BP was forced to buy on the spot market. This actually proved to be a positive, because BP was able to obtain the cheapest crude, push efficiency, and sharpen its entrepreneurial skills.

"The sale of power plants by the major utilities is analogous to BP losing its crude oil supply," writes Nichols. "Without power plants, companies have to buy power on the market to meet their customer demand. There's still a notion in the power market industry that one needs power plants to be a market participant. I've worked on this issue several times in my career. In New Zealand, we made the point that owning assets is not important in supplying customers or in making money. However, the New Zealand customer decided it was good at maintaining and operating thermal plants, so it kept the assets, based on its ability to create low-cost kilowatts.

"What are good reasons to have power generation in the U.S. power markets? The only one that comes to mind is the ability to dispatch and control output in order to meet hourly demand that is priced high. However, once I say this, some generator will construct some bilateral contract to give dispatch control to a trading company. The latter may be better able to value that contract and take on the peak pricing risk.

"I believe the next value step for marketers is to help utilities manage the difficulties in physical delivery, scheduling, planning, transportation, etc.

Yes, trading is good, but the higher value lies in participating in the difficult area of managing trading with ISO, or whatever one calls the central control center for transportation and reliability."

BACK TO THE FUTURE

There is incredible volatility in energy products, and there's a plethora of them. (BTU man gets to enjoy the products, but he also gets the pleasure of paying for them in terms of volatility.) Huge as the energy market of today is, however, it will be dwarfed by the emerging power market of tomorrow. And the market mechanics will be far from static.

Today's BTU merchant has to

- offer products that are still evolving

- to customers whose brand loyalties are disintegrating

- to a market that's still emerging

- via a technology that creates instant obsolescence

- through a governmental process that is deregulating

- working alongside and for those who are still learning how to manage their new tools and their projections.

If this individual truly believes he is in control of the market, then he also believes he's in control of the future.

THE EVOLVING OF THE INDEPENDENT

"Any fool can make a million dollars. Just not every fool can hang on to it."
—Tom Slick, known as King of the Wildcatters

The independent producer of oil and gas in America has never had to worry about a revolution. That's because he has been totally enmeshed in a senseless civil war with a country and its citizens. Those citizens have thrived on the product of his labors since that first well in 1859. Over the years, though, they have unilaterally developed rules of war dictating that he function unobtrusively, at no risk to anybody but himself, and for minimal profit. His consumer constituency must have his product, yet they fight him every inch of the way. On any given day, he has had to guess the issue *du jour* and adjust his anticipated conduct accordingly.

Despite his roller-coaster ride on the popularity polls, there's one thing he has always been able to count on. His government has never helped him out by paying him for his fields to lie fallow during periods of low prices.

Is that why he's called an independent? No. The name comes from a historical designation meant to indicate an upstream company, an exploration and production company (an E&P) that was *independent* of refiners and/or pipeliners. The vertically integrated companies that cover the landscape from far upstream all the way downstream to the retail outlets are dubbed the *majors*.

Historically, independents and majors have not been adversaries; they have functioned in a symbiotic relationship, like the classic analogy of the tick birds that helpfully feed off the annoying insects on the rhino's back.

The majors became the industry's landbanks–as large public companies, they had the financial resources to inventory large blocks of unexplored territory. (It was difficult for regulated financial institutions such as banks to perform this function.) The majors couldn't drill that vast acreage by themselves. They had to *farm* out–that is, have sample leasehold blocks explored and developed by others while retaining substantial ownership. The willing sharecroppers were the independents, most of whom had received their early training with majors, thus becoming very familiar with their corporate MOs. (Majors used to differ enormously from one to the other; now they are inbred to the point of a total lack of genetic diversity.)

This arrangement gave the independents the opportunity to explore and develop land they couldn't have afforded otherwise. It gave the majors two opportunities: to control and leverage their *domestic* production and to examine the emerging global potential, as political circumstances permitted, first in Mexico and South America, and then in the Middle East.

According to the Independent Petroleum Association of America (IPAA), there are as many as 8,000 E&Ps in North America. They range all the way from mom-and-pops with a couple of *stripper* wells (wells producing fewer than ten barrels of oil or oil equivalents per day) to giants such as Union Pacific Resources Group of Fort Worth, with its vast global reserves.

Two-thirds of the natural gas volume produced in North America is produced by independents. But how independent are they?

To understand the answer to that question, you must first meet the players who have always made up an independent company and see how they have evolved.

THE E&P PLAYERS

The *geologist*. He studies the surface and subsurface attributes of an area and maps a subsurface formation to determine the best location to find hydrocarbons, hopefully in commercial quantities.

The *geophysicist*. A computer nerd who was deprived of a pet rock in childhood, he can't map or draw, and is too introverted to become a geologist.

The *engineer*. This one guesstimates the amount of recoverable hydrocarbons in the prospective geological reservoir, and supervises the drilling and completion of the well and its production during its economic life. To paraphrase Mark Twain: "There are three kinds of lies: Lies, damn lies, and reservoir analyses."

The *landman*. He determines the mineral and surface ownership of the prospect, negotiates the leases, works with the regulatory bodies to determine the well drilling and spacing, makes the necessary regulatory filings, and then determines the division of interest for revenue payments throughout the life of the well, if it proves to be productive. His ethical code was too high for law practice.

The *marketer*. He is responsible for getting the wellhead product to the market as fast as he can, for as high a price as he can, with as few lies as he can.

The *lessor, mineral,* or *royalty owner*. This trio receives a percentage of the drilling and spacing unit's oil and gas production without bearing any of the costs of finding or producing the hydrocarbons. Originally, mineral ownership was the prerequisite of the king, who received a percentage of the precious metals mined in his realm. Today, the landowner thinks that he is king and that his land is gold.

The *nonoperated working interest owner*. He has a so-called working interest in the well derived from his partial ownership of an oil and gas lease in the drilling and spacing unit. This means that he is subject to all of the costs of drilling, completion and operation of the lease, but he is usually not the operator–because he got out-promoted somewhere in the prospect.

The *well operator*. He finds the deals. If he doesn't have any money, then he has to find partners. That makes him a promoter. If the lease is nowhere near existing production, then he's a wildcatter. If the wildcat well comes in as a major discovery, he becomes Wildcatter of the Year. If he can do this twice in his career, he becomes a rainmaker.

Why did these players work well together as an E&P team? Because from the days of the earliest wildcatter, success most often made those around them very wealthy.

It was never "the boss" but "we" drilling the well up in Beaver County. This camaraderie grew out of a device known as an *overriding royalty interest*. An ORRI is a non-working royalty interest–you don't pay any of the drilling, production, or operating costs associated with the well. It's assigned in a prospect as a form of bonus or participation in the success of the venture. Once an ORRI is assigned, the holder begins to think of the prospect differently. It's no longer just a prospect; it's a multimillion-dollar lottery ticket. To a wildcatter, every deal is a company-maker; to an ORRI holder, it is his ticket to retirement.

In the early days, as word spread of the wealth that could flow from the wildcatter's talents–and it was both the ease and the immensity of the wealth that lured–enrollment in geological and engineering schools swelled overnight. Another gold rush began–only it was black gold and centered in a different coast this time. The age of the Hydrocarbon Man had begun, and the era of the wildcatter took off. Southwestern states like Texas and Oklahoma were the fortunate beneficiaries of this newfound wealth, and oil men were their favorite sons.

In many cases the early-day oil man wasn't really all that smart. He just made lots of money. He became very wealthy by doing one thing particularly well. He found oil–and lots of it. And, as mentioned earlier, in some instances oil literally found him.

The legendary H. L. Hunt is a case in point. (Fig. 8-1) It has been said that he could find more oil with a roadmap than most geologists could with structure maps. He and his peers found and produced huge oil reserves without the benefit of the modern electric drilling rigs, earth satellite imagery, or three-dimensional seismic. The key assets often were enthusiasm and persistence in promoting ventures, obvious geological features (such as oil seeps, prominent surface faults, and anticlines), a lax regulatory environment, and a burgeoning demand for the product. His worst nightmare was drilling some dog that might bring less than a 50-to-1 return. The worst curse of all was finding natural gas instead of crude oil.

The early oil man was fortunate in that mineral interests in the United States have been owned in most cases by individual landowners rather than sovereign owners. The wildcatter and the landowner could come to terms fairly quickly; there was no intricate and time-consuming bureaucratic

Fig. 8-1 Wildcatter H. L. Hunt (with straw hat and cigar) is in good company here, in front of East Texas' Daisy Bradford #3. Fellow wildcatters Dad Joiner and Doc Lloyd (shaking hands) are joined by, among others, Glenn Pool (between Joiner and Lloyd). Pool brought in the oil strike that put Oklahoma on the map.

process. As a result, this became one of the few countries in the world without a national oil company, and without a nationalized oil industry.

Ironically, the oil man always complains that this country doesn't have a national energy policy. He's right. But we don't have a national oil company, either. The independent has been left alone. He didn't compete with the majors—in fact, he complemented the majors. Most importantly for him, as well as for the majors, there has not been a federal E&P company to preempt the private sector.

Today's Sacred Barometer

That's how they made money then. Those companies were predominantly private; today the midsized to large independents are predominantly public. Yesterday, individual success was rewarded if the well and prospect came in. Today, bonuses and stock options have largely replaced the ORRI;

where it exists, it's no longer assigned individually but in a pool. It's no longer how good the well is. It's what the analyst says the company is worth, or how high the stock price is. One well doesn't make or break personal success. Now one company geologist can drill nothing but dry holes as long as another company geologist hits a big one, so that everybody in the company shares in the rising stock price.

An ORRI is a percentage of ownership in a prospect and a share of stock is a percentage of ownership in a company. In a private company, the banker basically gets his loan back plus interest, but today the investment banker has become a pivotal player. Every time the majors shift their concentration overseas, the independents get a window of opportunity. When that happens, the capital markets respond. As with all public companies, the earnings-per-share (EPS) ratio is the sacred barometer. Energy is no exception. With capital markets flowing to the energy sector, today's investment banker and analyst scrutinize wildcat prospects of the future with the same interest as did the ORRI holders of the past.

THE SHRINKING TARGET

The company-makers of yesterday passed on their legacies to the future through impressive income streams that have lasted for decades. The work of that early-day wildcatter is still pretty evident in today's energy companies, which still operate many of these early discovery wells. Most of the names have changed, though, from Oil Company to Oil & Gas Company and on to the 1990s' Energy Company.

But as the wealth flowed onward, so did problems:

- a geologically shrinking universe

- a fairly constant price

- the environmental revolution

- the industry's concomitant despoiler image

THE WASTE OF RESOURCES

While the early-day oil boom found and recovered billions of barrels of oil in the United States, the producers' lack of knowledge (and regulatory control) combined with unbridled greed created many future problems.

The first large structures they discovered contained impressive virgin reservoir pressures. They also featured open-bore production that was unrestricted (unchoked) to control pressures. There were no established drilling and well-spacing units, and no prorationing of wells. These excesses bled off pressures and destroyed natural drive formations yet left much of the reservoir's oil still in place. (Primary production recovers only from 10% to 40% of the oil in place depending upon reservoir characteristics and conservation practices utilized.)

Needless to say, those early wells had enormous initial flow rates and the payouts and rates of returns (ROR) were quite impressive. These first discoveries were truly company-makers, providing the reserves for corporate growth.

But the oil patch operated at a hectic pace, with oil men having to make their money back to pay off their investors before the offsetting well drained their lease. Wells and fields depleted too quickly, and supply gluts all but ruined a once glorious party. State conservation commissions soon intervened with drilling and spacing units and prorationing to protect the correlative rights of offsetting interest owners. But the obvious targets had been hit hard.

Targets still exist, of course, but a great many are taboo. Most infamous are the controversial segments of the Alaska Natural Wildlife Reserve (ANWR) and offshore California. Yes, company-makers still exist. But not only are they in the Gulf of Mexico, they are in the Deep Gulf, where dry-hole costs reach up to $25 million. In most of North America, the less-expensive exploration has really become nothing more than exploitation.

Wells and fields that were once company-makers now have become depleting resources. Their owners scratch their heads over where to go next, in order to stay ahead of the reservoir depletion curve, and to continue to grow the company at historical rates. Should they look for areas with the largest known reserves but high acquisition cost? Or for the most potential formations to capitalize on a real serendipity and reduce risk? Or consider only current cost versus return by looking at the highest production for dollar spent–the shallow-versus-deep dilemma?

Or one can go abroad. A lot of companies (and not just the majors) have found overseas E&P very rewarding, companies such as Apache and Triton. But some, including majors, have been spectacularly burned. E&P abroad has its own distinctive problems that, unfortunately, surface only after much expenditure.

THE CONSTANT PRICE

The product price in real dollars has remained fairly constant at $15-$25 per barrel, regardless of demand or supply, since Colonel Drake's 1859 discovery well. Successive administrations in Washington have made it totally clear that the price of oil, gas, and gasoline must stay "affordable." That is, it's perfectly appropriate for more than 50% of the U.S. crude supply to come from abroad, and if this supply is threatened, the United States will go to war.

Every time the U.S. public is hit with higher prices at the gasoline pump or the factory gate, it goes ballistic and screams at its elected representatives or takes to manufacturing outlandish conspiracy theories. What the U.S. public never does is compare what it pays to ensure supplies from elsewhere in the world with the tab it has been so graciously picking up as the world's Middle East security force. Factor in those costs and a barrel of crude or a gallon of gasoline comes to considerably more than what you pay at the pump. Actually, gasoline engenders a two-part payment. You pay X amount per gallon when you fill 'er up, and the rest on April 15 with your 1040 filing.

Because of this price constancy, early-day companies relied upon growth through the drill bit–that is, replacing reserves faster than they depleted them.

While there has always been spiking of commodity prices due to war and shortages, few have been able to predict such occurrences very far in advance with any impressive degree of accuracy. Neither do many realists confess to relying upon the hope of constantly escalating prices and inflation. After all, hope is the enemy of a rational trader.

According to Michael C. Lynch of MIT, "The many lamentations about the long-term availability of resources are completely misguided. No mineral has ever 'run out,' nor has any mineral ever experienced long-term rising price trends. In fact, the primary resource problems in modern times have, ironically enough, stemmed from the depletion of *renewable* resources like fish and trees."

THE STIGMA

The environmental revolution struck just as the rapidly growing population became more urban, more detached from the underpinnings that make a lot of its lifestyle possible. It became more inclined to view what it now calls "the outdoors" as a playground rather than as the source of basic commodities.

Everybody is an environmentalist in the sense that nobody is in favor of pollution. Indeed, most people are finger-pointing environmentalists, in that they judge their ancestors by today's standards.

Wildcat fever is contagious. The thrill of bringing in a well is an experience that is difficult to describe and practically impossible to ever really get out of an oil man's blood. In the early days, if drilling a well was a difficult experience to forget, plugging a dry or depleted well was even more difficult to remember. Ugly scars began to dot the landscape. As urban sprawl and the yuppie migration back to rural America made abandoned wells even more visible, the industry's negative image plummeted farther. The environmentalist hue and cry to clean up these dangerous eyesores was soon joined by all sectors of the American public.

When the 1970s introduced the TV show *Dallas* with J.R. Ewing as the oil man everybody loved to hate, the show's global ratings soared, and the image of the oil man hit new lows.

Excess, greed, and corruption became the identifying traits. Oil embargoes, long lines at the gasoline pumps, and, of course, high energy prices made long-lasting imprints on the minds of consumers. Those high prices didn't stay around for very long, but the negative image did.

Ironically, despite the image created by J.R. Ewing, most independent producers were men of great honor and integrity. Their core values centered on the fact that their word was their bond, and that a handshake was as good as any contract written. This proved to be especially true after a decade of independents' take-or-pay natural gas contracts were walked on by pipelines in the 1980s. Now a key member of any E&P team is a lawyer.

It is very difficult to find any living form of humanity that will publicly condone the defiling of Mother Earth. Unfortunately, it is equally difficult to find many forms of individual or corporate life on the same planet that will offer to voluntarily pay for restitution. So who pays?

Anybody who appears in the chain of title for an environmentally suspect lease will probably be the recipient of some really thought-provoking correspondence (registered, of course). And this brings up an interesting question. Can any but a very large independent afford the potential environmental and abandonment liabilities associated with future well operations?

HOW TO GROW?

So, faced with a geologically shrinking universe, a basically unvarying commodity price, a rotten image, and a hefty environmental responsibility, independents tussle with the nagging dilemma of growth. In a world of a depleting resource, replacement becomes hypercritical.

Let's eavesdrop on the independent as he strategizes, out loud.

"How do I keep my track record intact and stay attractive to the investment community? Well, I can create an economy of scale by concentrating in an area where I already have operations and field personnel and just concentrate on my core competencies. I can improve technology by making my hydrocarbons cheaper to find and produce…

"That's it! I'll become a low-cost producer! I can utilize portfolio management by selling off marginal properties that cost too much to operate and produce too little income, and use those funds to drill more wells with greater potential. I can explore the possibilities of enhanced secondary recovery on some of my fields that are at the end of their economic life.

"I can shift my exploration efforts to offshore or internationally–yeah, like Kerr-McGee. They drilled that first offshore well 50 years ago, and now they're strictly offshore and in the South China Sea. Used to be an independent, then they were a major, and now they're an independent again.

"I can become a better marketer of my product in the spot market and get more for my product than those other guys doing long-term forward contracting. After all, everyone knows the price is just going to continue to go up and I sure as hell don't want to give away the upside.

"Shucks, maybe I'll form my own marketing co-op just like the farmers…

"Maybe I'll cash out and move to a basin with better transportation and marketing ops. What do we call it now?… Monetize. Yes! Redeploy my cash flow where it works better for me.

"Okay, so the spot market can be a little volatile. I guess risk-management is the way of the future. I can find less expensive investment money that will enhance my ROR–but which source? Conventional energy banking, mezzanine financing, investment bankers, public offerings…those good ol' industry promotes like third for a quarter?…

"What to do? I know one thing, with all these SEC and accounting filings, I never have time to find oil and gas."

"OK, maybe I should do an acquisition–what are we calling them now? An A&D, right, acquisitions and divestitures. Problem is, I've got to figure out how to target prospects. I've also got to figure out what altitude to look at the target from–50,000 feet or ground zero. Devon did it right–hell of a deal buying Kerr-McGee's onshore properties!

"'Course, Kerr-McGee now owns a big chunk of Devon…"

MIGRATION PATH

So what's the upstream player's migration path? What does he see when he looks at the industry's midstream and downstream? Will the upstream player decide to let the current take him–and will he drown trying to swim downstream? Is it true that only dead fish float downstream?

There is one inescapable fact: The product that the upstream player brings to market cannot be replaced. Not even the most ardent environmentalist hell-bent on returning this country to an agrarian society will argue the necessity of the product that fuels his allegedly simple life. Therefore, the oil and gas finder is hardly likely to disappear from the planet.

But that isn't the point. The point, the paramount question, has become how does the independent continue to grow a company? More importantly, how can anyone ever start a brand new energy company from scratch?

The two choices still remain the drill bit or acquisition. If you are a public company, how is growth measured and by whose expectations? The energy analysts have become the corporate watchdogs for the industry as they analyze quarterly reports, crunch the numbers, and issue their much-revered, closely followed opinions.

These opinions, which can be invaluably helpful or very damaging, can cause great volatility in share prices. This volatility in turn affects the corporation's market capitalization, and this affects the delicate balance between debt and equity. Oddly enough, just as engineers can take the same well and production data and arrive at wide variations in value, so analysts can evaluate the same corporate strategies, talk with the same key executives, and analyze the same data to come up with vastly different opinions. The industry calls their work "opinions," because that is exactly what an analyst's work is–his opinion of a company's financial health and all of the internal and external factors that may continue to enhance or harm its future well-being.

So what catches analysts' attention?

They use various gauges including a ratio of debt and equity to cash flow, a growth in earnings, the reserve growth per share, growth by drill bit or by acquisition, management savvy compared to peers, good fundamentals with low-risk profiles, or newer industry measures, such as EVA (economic value added) that examines return on capital employed.

What are the red flags to watch for?

For Paul Leibman at Petrie Parkman & Co., it's high debt, poor reserve replacement, high finding costs, lack of strategic focus, and negative economics of underlying assets. M. Carole Coale at Prudential Securities, Inc. watches for high debt related to acquisitions. Lawrence A. Crowley, CFA at Jefferies & Co. Inc., is perturbed by high leverage, high cost of operations, and lack of strategic overview.

You have seen how deregulation has been breaking up and continues to break up the little boxes that used to contain and restrain the various forms of energy. You have also seen how energy is becoming more and more of a commodity–and commodities are by definition volatile–and how today's consumer is in almost total control of the energy market, although he is almost totally unaware of his power.

So against this background, you're an upstream player trying to decide how to deal with geology, the environment, the image, the market, and the omnipotent BTU consumer. Assuming you still want to be an upstream player, where's the money coming from? Who's in control?

HERE'S YOUR ANSWER

The question at the beginning of this chapter was how independent are the independents? Well, the smart, forward-thinking ones have become more financially independent than they used to be. They're more genetically diversified than they used to be, as fewer of them have come up through the majors' ranks. As many independents now come out of financial institutions as come out of E&P training grounds. The independent's evolutionary process has been such that he can now work with many different segments besides the majors. He can be all things to all people. And he has reassessed old relationships with new opportunities.

So, the independents with ideas are thinking forward while looking backward. They agree with Damon Runyon that, "The race isn't always to the swift nor the battle to the strong, but that's the way to bet it." They also know that, if you haven't had time to do your homework and handicap your horses, a familiar jockey with a proven track record will still get your horse in the winner's circle.

So, looking backward, the thinking independent sees a jockey with a proven track record. None other than the service and supply companies, the S&S boys, the old face who can play a new role.

THE S&S SOLUTION

These companies were among the early beneficiaries of the early-day oil men. They benefited from his successes while they remained the unglamorous part of the industry, the plumbers of the oil patch. How many TV series do you think were made about Bubba's Rathole Service?

But it was the service and supply boys who floated the oil man credit on a regular basis and, more importantly, from boom to bust. By the early '70s, some of the oilfield plumbers had gotten really industry-savvy and gone from local- to regional- to national-size to meet the needs of the growing independent. The industry paid attention to the emergence of Eddie Chiles and The Western Company, and everybody in the oil patch sported his bumper sticker, *If you don't have an oil well, get one!*

The service and supply crowd had climbed the ladder of acceptance and prestige. The boom was on, and the S&S man was now an invited and welcome guest to all of the oil man's events—and not just to cook the fish or barbecue the cabrito. The S&S man really earned his way into the oil man's world. He was always a quiet partner in the credit risk, and now companies such as Halliburton, Schlumberger, Baker Hughes, BJ Services, and Western Atlas Logging are full—and logical—partners in the profit.

That is one of three relationships that have evolved into opportunities—the other two being the midstream and the downstream. Your smarter independent, instead of continuing to duke it out with the players in these industry sectors, has become opportunistic. He has realized that new opportunities often need new partners. In other words, if you can't fight 'em, promote 'em.

An upstream player doesn't just borrow money from a bank—he rents the money for an anticipated ROR. When a speculator invests, he doesn't want a respectable ROR—he wants obscene multiples because he's in it for the big commodity play. Neither bank nor speculator is in it for the commodity itself, but the bank cares about the company because it wants relationship business. The speculator is impersonal; he wants a rapidly appreciating commodity–cattle, gold, copper, whatever. All he cares about is the action and the score. He wants to make the point spread, to win big. The typical speculator doesn't even watch the game or really care about the players. So if times go bad or the investment turns sour, he wants his money back. He doesn't want the cheese–he just wants out of the trap.

The S&S, the player in the gathering-processing-marketing (GPM) sector, the burnertip investor (a utility or industrial end user)...they all know the best place to find the cheese is in the trap. It's a mutually beneficial relationship. The S&S keeps its equipment and personnel working; the GPM gets the product it needs; the burnertip gets its fuel source.

This new relationship tears down barriers, allowing the upstream to look all the way downstream. The independent producer of the hydrocarbon era did not follow his product once it got picked up; that was the posted-price mentality.

As Merrill Lynch analyst John Olson notes, it was at this point that the producer lost control of the commodity. These days, the independent needs to look all the way across the value stream and make sure that his partners do well. The profitability of what used to be an adversarial sector of the industry or of a business segment outside the oil industry is now very much part of the independent's profitability.

Then the question becomes this: As necessity forces the various sectors of the industry to break down barriers and learn each other's cultures, will the corporate egos force each other to cross-pollinate.

Better yet...*can* they?

THE CHANGING OF THE GUARD

"His education cost fifty million dollars and all he learned was how to subtract."
— Robert Gregory, *Oil in Oklahoma*

1982: It was the best of times, it was the worst of times.

Penn Square Bank, NA was a small bank with very big dreams. Located in the back corner of a fashionable shopping center in an affluent suburb of Oklahoma City, the bank's owner had a grandiose plan. He wanted to become the premier energy merchant bank in the world. Actually, his plan wasn't all that bad, but considering that he lacked the risk-management tools available today, his judgment and timing were poor, to say the least.

It has always seemed that energy prices and the industry are never quite in sync with the rest of the country. The boom years of the '70s and '80s were no exception. The lumber industry in the Pacific Northwest, the automotive industry in the Midwest, real estate in the Northeast, foreign loans to South America…all were experiencing a downturn. Major regional banks like Seattle First National Bank, Michigan National Bank of Lansing, Northern Trust Company of Chicago, and Chase Manhattan Bank all desperately needed new downstream-origination sources for their loan portfolios.

Penn Square was soon to become the quick financial fix. It had some $2 billion of new energy loans available for immediate participation with the right upstream counterpart. The Penn Square customer base had grown quickly and included some very substantial borrowers.

Fig. 9-1 Oklahoma City's Penn Square Bank on the day following its close at the hands of federal regulators. The institution was about to become the epicenter of an earthquake that rippled throughout the energy and banking sectors. (Photo from the Daily Oklahoman, used by permission)

To maintain liquidity, the bank had paid very high CD rates to attract very large depositors.

THE ECLIPSE

Sunday, July 4, 1982 was a typically beautiful, hot, and sunny Fourth of July. At a celebration at the exclusive Oak Tree Country Club in Edmond, Oklahoma–an affluent suburb of Oklahoma City–local oil men gathering to play in the annual Flag Tournament discussed the bank examiners sent in by the comptroller of the currency to once again examine Penn Square's energy-lending portfolio.

Visits by bank examiners had become about as frequent in Oklahoma City as oil-man tourists to Cancun, but their seemingly endless presence was beginning to cause nervous controversy. Still, most tournament participants were quite smug about their bank's solvency and the status of their energy loans. There was some talk about the next day's full lunar eclipse, but nobody at that tournament expected a total financial version.

A great day of playing to one's inflated handicap and good-ol'-boy back-slapping came to an end as the golfers were joined by their families for an Okie-style Oilie BBQ–you know, bigger and better than can be found in Texas–and some spectacular fireworks.

The real fireworks would begin the following day.

On the evening of July 5, the FDIC chairman and other senior officials left Washington on private jets, headed for Oklahoma City–and not for a round of golf at Oak Tree. Penn Square officials and their depositors had learned only a few hours before the jets' departure–fittingly, as the earth began to eclipse the moon–that the comptroller of the currency had declared Penn Square Bank insolvent. As the eclipse lifted and the sun came out, Penn Square was reopened under the supervision of the FDIC.

THE BANK TO BEAT–AND TO BAIL

During this time of overreaching, the major bank that was most aggressive in its energy lending was Continental Illinois National Bank and Trust Company, then the largest money-center bank in the Midwest and seventh largest in the nation. When it came to energy lending, *The Wall Street Journal* called Continental Illinois "the bank to beat."

When energy prices began to weaken and Penn Square was subsequently closed, it became clear that Continental Illinois, with its huge portfolio of energy loans from Penn Square and other energy banks, was in serious trouble.

In 1984, two years after Penn Square's collapse, there was a global run on the bank as other banks and companies pulled their money out. Penn Square's demise had caused numerous banks to close but none of them were of the magnitude of Continental Illinois. The integrity of the entire interconnected banking system was now in serious jeopardy.

After reviewing the possible consequences and determining there was no other choice, the federal government intervened with a huge bailout that included $8 billion in emergency loans, $5.5 billion in new capital, and new management. Continental Illinois, had in effect, been nationalized. Needless to say, energy lending was no longer in vogue. E&P capital dried up. The boom was over; the bust had begun.

As a result of this last bust, the energy industry eventually lost more than half a million *career* individuals, give or take a few hundred. Most of these individuals were specially, professionally trained. With their going, the industry didn't lose its J.R. Ewing image or its environmental liabilities, and the hydrocarbons are still in the ground. What the industry lost was talent across the board. T.S. Eliot's plaint comes to mind: "Where is all the knowledge that was lost in the information? Where is all the wisdom that was lost in the knowledge?"

The young–those for whom the oil patch was a legacy and a future–suffered the largest casualties. As a result, the industry has suffered a generation skip. The loss lay in its junior officers. When it came time for them to assume command, they weren't there. Drilling rig or battleship, it's hard to operate a 24-hour duty tour without reliable relief. Natural gas is a unique commodity because it will expand to fill any void, and just like natural gas, the industry made do–but the loss is no more real.

LEADERSHIP ROLE

Today, there's no shortage of available money, but a shortage of intellectual capital is a matter of concern.

As Lou Pai, chief operating officer at Enron Capital & Trade, cautions: "At Enron there is no shortage of opportunities. What we worry about is a shortage of talent to evaluate the opportunities."

Enron isn't alone in noticing. In May 1997, at the Offshore Technical Conference in Houston, the 36,000 attendees from 80 countries viewed the qualified-personnel shortage as a very stiff challenge. "The issue is, 'Why do they not see our industry is an attractive place to work?'" said Exxon Company International executive vice president Stuart McGill. "The damage that we've done to ourselves as a career industry is the single biggest barrier that we've got."

Bemoaned Noble Drilling president James C. Day: "Right now people are robbing from one another. It's going to be a problem."

This talent shortage has led to a scramble that's causing corporate to spend practically as much time looking for talent as for hydrocarbons. Necessity has forced the search into other industries, especially those (such as telecommunications) that offer the promise of real help with electricity deregulation. But there really isn't a solid replacement for the younger professional, bred into the oil patch, whose career was intelligently and deliberately moving toward a leadership role. And an oil patch legacy is no mere sentiment and clubbishness. Without a sense of the past, there's often no insightful reading of the future.

So, in today's energy industry, there is no cadre of suitable replacements. Add to this the fact that the leader is more tired than he probably realizes. He has been on that deck a very long time, and thanks to downsizing he doesn't get to delegate much—even if he ever knew how or wanted to.

Consider the Goose Factor. When geese fly in formation, the leader heads the flight. When the leader tires, he takes a temporary position at the tail of the flight. The leader goose lives within a system that has both the tradition and the existence of a reliable relief, which probably arose in the antiquity of the genus because the alternative was to fly only part way, or crash from vertigo.

In today's energy industry—as well as corporate America in general—there is no such tradition. In fact, if the goose world were like corporate America, leader geese would lead until, in utter exhaustion, they led the whole flight into the ground (at which point we would naturally pay the fallen leader big bucks as part of his severance package).

So the industry's generation skip is unfortunately complicated by the presence in the industry of egos that are larger than life. Remember, huge egos are a role requirement in a business born of the wildcatter's irrepressible enthusiasm and aggressiveness. Their philosophy matches Confederate General Nathan Bedford Forrest's philosophy: "Get there first with the most."

FEAR, EGO, AND GREED

The driving factors in every company are *fear, ego,* and *greed.* On any given day, they are either your best friends or your worst nightmares. They make up your worst nightmare when they are allowed to get out of control like an Orange County or a Barings Bank debacle. They are your best friends when they are understood and channeled into positive energy and market savvy within a corporation. It takes a leader, and not a tired ego, to understand and channel, focus and inspire the company–especially in the absence of reliable junior officers.

Just as in bottles, corporate bottlenecks are always found at the top of the bottle. Top management's emotional equity is most often invested in the past. Typically, the energy corporation's senior leaders tend to be the least imaginative, have the least contact with the markets they serve, and share the least genetic diversity of any level of management within a company.

While most take pride in the corporation's asset accumulation and management under their helm, most fail to pay very close attention to their company's depreciating intellectual capital base. And to top things off, the leader's ego–a healthy one to start–has been stoked by the very fact of the leader's survival in a brutal downturn.

Is this man in a position to cross-pollinate his ego with those of his new midstream and downstream partners as he exerts true leadership for his company?

Are we going to look up someday and see ducks and geese flying together?

No. But believe it or not, hope does exist in the new energy world. Even as recently as five years ago, would anybody in the oil patch have expected to see upstream, midstream, and downstream partnering each other?

The real purpose of the leader goose is to lessen wind resistance for his followers in the formation in which they fly. As the visionary and navigator, he provides the sense of direction. He sets not only the course but also its pace, and he selects the formation's resting stops as well as their timing and duration. He shows a sense of purpose and balance. He eschews corporate jets.

Offhand, the only similarity that springs to mind between the goose and the corporate leader is that both head south for the winter.

Nonetheless, be it fowl goose or corporate goose, the correct and timely migration path becomes an important part of the species' survival process.

CREATING WEALTH

Senior management's primary purpose–in any organization–is to create wealth for the organization's shareholders. By developing a framework for creating wealth, senior management must create a migration path to transition the company and its business into the future, because a company that's not replacing reserves or otherwise showing sustained growth is in effect in liquidation.

Without such a migration path, the cynic's belief comes to pass. Corporations have three generations of leadership–the creators, the administrators, and the undertakers.

The energy industry has always been cyclical in nature, lurching from boom to bust. Neither calamity lasts forever, thank God, but the point of a correct and timely migration path is that it helps the corporation weather the cycles better.

Drilling rigs come equipped with blow-out preventers (BOP) and numerous control panels with all kinds of alarms and warning lights; unfortunately, corporate boardrooms are not nearly as well-equipped. Maybe someone should invent an ego BOP.

Sooner or later tomorrow becomes today, and yesterday's visionary foresight becomes the conventional wisdom of the day. Successful migration paths must have the necessary trail markers that will differentiate between trends and fads. The leader should ask, "Are we constantly improving and innovating, or just following the rest of the herd?" He should caution that prematurely abandoning a potential migration path is just as hazardous as prematurely committing to the wrong one and not altering the course soon enough. Both decisions are an unfortunate manifestation of corporate ego.

It is difficult to discuss leadership in any detail without examining the side effects associated with ego. A healthy ego–in check and under control–can help the corporation to excel and to pass its competitors both in market share and in earnings. As the saying goes, "That's what makes a good horserace."

What happens when the corporate egos run loose?

While egos are often very noticeable and at times very difficult to hide, how do we measure or audit corporate egos, or equate them into dollars on a balance sheet?

How do the analysts follow corporate egos? And finally, do corporate egos get in the way of progress and opportunity?

When considering an M&A deal, for instance, is the consideration whether the deal is good for the directors, for the senior management team, for the investment bankers, or for the shareholders?

"Oh well," as they say in the brokerage business, "three out of four ain't bad."

Do egos get in the way of the courage to act? Consider the case of the utilities coming out of the shelter of years of regulation. They have steadily paid increasing and expected dividends to demanding shareholders. Will management have the guts to make the unpopular decision to cut or suspend the expected and coveted dividends and divert the capital for the utility's growth?

Management must have the courage to become rule breakers instead of rule followers.

"Essentially, there are two ways to add value to a company," cautions Price Waterhouse's World Petroleum Industry Group. "Reduce the amount of money flowing out of the corporation or increase the amount of money coming in. Cut costs or add revenues. Business process reengineering has been widely praised as an effective tool for adding value to oil and gas companies. But does it add value by cutting costs or increasing revenues? If reengineering succeeds only in reducing costs, its potential is limited. But if it creates opportunities leading to new, profitable revenues, its promise is great."

WHO'S THE NAVIGATOR?

So who charts the path and puts up the trail signs?

Will a generation skip inevitably lead to an intellectual gap?

Are we heading toward another mutiny on the Bounty?

Will this be an era of cooperation, or will old age and treachery overcome youth and skill?

Is this to be the era of the tail wagging the dog, perhaps?

Will this be the Graybeards vs. Generation X? It's a focus that has already led to frequent downsizings, followed by yet another slate of inexperienced players. Perhaps the ultimate compromise may be to allow Generation X to be the corporate visionaries while the Graybeards utilize their experience to become the catalyst for change.

A favorite Oklahoma oil patch story tells of a very rich oil man and his maturing son. On the son's all-important 21st birthday, as an award of manhood, the oil man presents him with a gift of $15 million. The son immediately purchases a yacht and invites all of his friends, close and otherwise, for a celebratory cruise. After successfully crossing half the globe, the vessel is approaching her berthing slot in Madrid when the captain, in a drunken stupor along with the rest of the crew and passengers, forgets to shut down the engines and drop anchor. The yacht crashes into the pier and sinks. Fortunately all aboard are able to stumble safely ashore.

At this point, not wanting to waste a perfectly good $5 million champagne buzz, the son purchases a Lear jet to continue the celebratory escapade. While approaching Miami International for a refueling stop, the captain, again celebrating with crew and passengers, forgets to set down the landing gear, for an embarrassing and career-ending landing.

At this point, the much poorer and wiser son decides to end his frivolous global fling. However, having met the love of his life on the fortuitous sojourn in Miami, he immediately proposes marriage and she, with love, lust, and greed in her eyes, accepts. Two weeks later she sues for divorce and prevails.

The son–heartbroken, money-broken, and just plain dejected in general–goes back to the calm serenity of his father's estate anticipating the wrath of one very angry old oil man. After summoning all of the courage to be found in a 21-year-old hungover body, the son spills his guts in fear.

The father listens with the wisdom of all fathers before him, smiles and asks, "And what did you learn, son?"

He replies, "Not a damn thing, sir. I just pissed away $15 million." Says the oil man, "No, son, you learned one of the most important lessons of life at a very early age. If it flies, floats, or fornicates–lease, don't buy."

WHO'S THE NEW GUARD?

We have spent a good deal of time examining current industry leaders. The conclusion is that a lot of talent, knowledge, and even wisdom were lost in the last energy bust; the industry is suffering a generation skip; and egos die hard.

In examining the next generation of leaders, the industry faces a very difficult changing of the guard, difficult for today's leadership to accept. If today's leaders have had a difficult time sharing quality time at home with their children while enduring rap and heavy metal music, they're going to love sharing the boardrooms of the future with their children's peers.

Youth is a wonderful phenomenon, because it is not yet trained to assess risk, and it rarely recognizes fear. But are guts born of inexperience necessarily a good thing? After all, Nick Leeson spent several years risking several billion dollars of Barings' money without bothering to notify his management. No big deal. What's a couple of billion dollars and the collapse of a centuries-old financial institution among friends, family, and colleagues?

But, once caught, he immediately knew that he had done something to displease his immediate superior. His last communication, before he went on the lam for several months in Germany: "I doubt that we'll be talking much in the future."

On the flip side of the organization chart, the young are viewed as an expendable commodity. A company never lacks for employment applications at the entry level. Because of their abundant numbers, they serve as prime scapegoats. This is especially true as senior management's increasingly fragile and exposed necks are constantly on the line to maximize shareholder value. Curiously, in sports, the owner fires the coach; in the energy world, he fires the team. The question arises: How many teams can companies afford to fire, hire, train, fire, hire, train, and so on?

One of the great paradoxes of the industry is that you always want to borrow money from the most inexperienced lender while buying prospects from the most seasoned geologist. Unfortunately, this next industry cycle looks like one of seasoned lenders and inexperienced geologists. The industry may not be able to find and extract either the oil or the money.

Who's Running the Show?

An energy company whose leader is a leader in name only is really in trouble because, as we have seen, more often than not controls range from poorly defined to poorly exercised.

In Chapter 4, the shareholder was described as the sunshine patriot, but he also deserves another moniker. He's the absentee landlord, who takes but doesn't give. What today's shareholder almost never gives is his attention. If shareholders are not attentively watching the CEO and his course of action, and the CEO isn't really running the company, he's CEO by default. And a CEO who's not running the show is running away from it.

If a share of stock represents a percentage of ownership in a company, why aren't company shareholders more interested in the companies they invest in?

What percentage of proxies sent out is ever returned?

How many attend annual shareholder meetings?

For the most part, shareholders are very passive investors. Then, who runs the companies? There's no mystery as to whom benefits—just take a close look at executive salaries and perks, not to mention the infamous golden parachutes. But who *runs* them? To whom has the shareholder abdicated his overseer responsibility?

He's abdicated to the most powerful class of individuals outside the corporation—the analyst. Let's look at him, and a trio of other spin doctors.

SECTION IV:
THE TRAVEL AGENTS

THE SPIN DOCTORS

"Power is the narcotic of the rich."
—John Ehrlichman

What do investment bankers, corporate analysts, lawyers, and consultants have in common?

Not much, if you're looking at all of the thousands and thousands of individuals in those occupations.

But carved out of all of these is a largely invisible inner circle–the kingmakers. And they have everything in common, their nature, motivation, function, and tools.

This relatively small group lives in a unique and rarefied ecosystem. They are neither predators nor parasites; they are the managers of the jungle, and their clients are its denizens. The clients' needs are simple–how to gain power and wealth, and how to hold on to both. The managers keep the jungle whole, and they keep the ecosystem clean and functional. The ecosystem has an exquisitely delicate balance; no predator or parasite can take such a big bite that the balance is skewed. So the managers orchestrate. Like conductors, they bring all the musicians together to make the harmonious music, keep the performance going, keep the public happy, keep the money flowing.

Theirs is a difficult job that requires some Machiavellian policing to keep the power equilibrium steady and make their clients presentable to the public. In this world, the end always justifies the means. To some, that may be one harsh world indeed, but kingmaking is a tremendously satisfying job for individuals of this nature.

What *is* the kingmakers' nature? Their brains are the analytical, far-sighted kind; they are realists about everything, starting with their own limitations. Supreme manipulators, they do not delude themselves. They know what the outcome has to be, and they make it happen. As Deputy Mayor Calhoun says in *City Hall*, "You've got to be willing to be lucky." These people are extremely competitive and need the trappings of wealth and power, but they do not thirst for the acclaim of the great, unwashed masses. And they know that they wield their power best if they remain in the background. As a result, they are seen and recognized by very few outside the boardrooms and other seats of power.

The kingmakers are the molders, shapers, and overseers of all the world's wealth; the CEOs, public or private, and government leaders cannot function without them. They are the Sherpas who guide them up the pinnacles of power. We can all name most of the world's political leaders, but can we name their Sherpas? They would find it both surprising and disconcerting if the man in the street knew their names. The Sherpas at the highest levels of the business world are even more obscure. All Sherpas have to have it that way. If nothing else, once their roles are known, their motives can be questioned in the media, homes, and workplaces. And the kingmakers will not subject themselves to questioning by the man in the street.

Their motivation does not impel them toward high elective office. It does impel them toward the acquisition, use, and retention of power, and toward sustained profit; they are not after one-time shots. They are the ultimate puppet masters. The strings they pull descend from high in the theater down to the puppets on stage. One of their puppets is the promoter. (The promoter then pulls the strings that lead to the public–but that's the next chapter.) The kingmakers need the promoter–he's their opening act that charms the crowd and sets the mood for their headline act.

HELLO, SUCKER!

Just as a trader doesn't make money in a flat market, the kingmakers need action.

Just as market direction doesn't matter to a trader as long as he has frequent and measurable volatility, the kingmakers need a world they can manipulate and control.

They need a shifting horizon; level playing fields are for regulated markets. There's always more money to be made with deregulation than in the status quo of regulation. As travel agents, they realize that the shortest distance between two points is hardly ever the most profitable.

With deregulation, they can take a sleepy little company and reshape it and its components; by recasting the entity and its players to meet the outcome they deem desirable, they can create wealth. And because they are so instrumental in the *process* of deregulation, they can rearrange the wealth of the world in their clients' favor–and do so in the name of the consumer.

That's why they're called spin doctors.

One of Oklahoma's most colorful politicians and trial attorneys once said that if you walk into a card game and you don't see a sucker sitting at the table, then you're probably it.

One would certainly be hard pressed to see a sucker sitting at the BTU spin doctors' table. So, it becomes intuitively obvious to even the most casual sucker that, if you're the sucker and they're the spin doctors, you clearly want to be on their side.

It is at this precise moment that the most frightening and thought-provoking question of all time begins to form: Exactly what side are they on?

Now We Call It Spin

"As Mark Twain once said, 'there are three sides to every story: Your side, my side, and the facts,'" remembers Washington columnist Doug Thompson.

He goes on to note, "In a political world, nobody ever loses a debate or an election. As soon as the speeches stop and before the votes are even counted, the TV cameras point toward some 'spokesman' who says his or her candidate 'sharpened their position' or 'clarified the issues' or 'defined the message' or 'stopped our opponent's momentum.' Not too long ago, this was called 'lying through your teeth.' Now its called spin.

"Spin means never having to say you're sorry, or wrong, or a loser. Spin is what the handlers use to try and explain away a lost primary vote, an incredibly stupid statement or a faltering campaign. Spin is taking the Big Lie and trying to make it sound like less of a lie."

How did we end up with spin? According to Thompson, "Spin exists because the mainstream media, in the guise of fairness, allows any nitwit with a connection to a campaign the ability to proclaim the carefully crafted 'position' of the campaign. That position usually has nothing to do with the facts. But then the facts may be the one side that never gets told in today's spin-infested world."

It is the Sherpas among the investment bankers, corporate analysts, lawyers, and consultants who are the BTU world's ultimate spin doctors. These are the sharp-suited, sharp-intellect professionals who originate the sound bites that are fed to the media, and who defuse negative issues and promote positive ones with their opinions, behind-the-scenes briefings, public statements, and interpretations. They are the ones who are in constant communication with the CEOs, the regulatory commissions and, in short, anyone shaping public or private energy policy. The BTU spin doctors are the strong invisible undercurrent that moves the traffic on the BTU value stream.

But in whose best interest? And who pays every time the BTU spin doctors operate?

CONTROLLING THE SPIN CYCLE

Spin doctors are a necessary function. They are not evil sorcerers. They provide many of the checks and balances that are vital in today's huge profit engines; they keep these engines fine-tuned. They are invaluable because today's financial machines are globally intertwined, all the more so because of today's instantaneous and transparent information. E-mail has replaced the three-month transoceanic reply. Global marketing demands timely reply and decision-making.

The spin doctors are the ones with the resources, experience, expertise, and incentive to keep the process moving and the ecosystem flourishing. As in politics, their work is the art of the possible. Their work is carried out in a self-contained system, where solving one client's problems provides solutions to other clients' problems. The system feeds on its very interrelated nature, its co-mingling, its incest.

Somebody has to orchestrate the process. The spin doctors have the intellectual capital for this orchestration; they have become the intellectual banks of the BTU world. They have been the beneficiaries of all the BTU world's "right-sizings," after all. If a company is serious about finding the perfect migration path, the perfect spin doctors are there for that company.

And whether it's the investment banker creating the right financing vehicle, the corporate analyst performing the acutely inspired analyses and projections, the lawyer shielding and sheltering via the adroit contract, or the consultant providing the best breakthrough thinking, the insatiable demand for retained expertise has stunned even the suppliers. Just ask one of the men at the head of the knowledge-capital parade. George T. Shaheen, CEO of Andersen Consulting, has seen his firm grow at the meteoric rate of more than 22% a year for the past three years. It currently employs more than 45,000 internationally. Its New York-based Financial Ideas Exchange is a symbol of the knowledge capital that will be tomorrow's business currency. In the words of *Chief Executive* magazine, Andersen Consulting is an "advice machine" that leads an industry that has been growing by more than 10% a year for the past seven years to a $20-billion-a-year industry.

Who are some of the others vying for a piece of this $20 billion dollar pie? Names like McKinsey & Co.; EDS; A.T. Kearney; Pricewaterhouse Coopers; Ernst & Young; Deloitte & Touche; KPMG Peat Marwick; Booz, Allen & Hamilton; Gemini; Boston Consulting Group; Arthur D. Little; Bain & Co., and Mercer Management Consulting claim the largest share of the BTU outsourcing dollars. And those are just the consultants.

The size of the ecosystem and the enormity of power in the hands of the BTU doctors on any given day are staggering. They are also sobering, giving rise to the question, "Who controls the spinners?" Beyond market forces and professional codes, they basically control each other through a self-imposed and very disciplined canon of conduct–conduct unbecoming a member of the spin club, conduct that can bring it all crashing down. They all have to play together, but at the end of the day, they cannot simply divide up all the toys and take them home. Because their businesses and clients are so intertwined, they can't grab more than their share. They have such a vested interest in the toys that they work like a self-regulating organization.

As in hockey, basketball, or soccer, the players have to bring the ball forward by passing. It is rare for an individual to advance the ball and score single-handed. Assists all the way, right? A good team player like Michael Jordan has more than physical gifts; he is a strategist. Moving down the court, he cannot run over his own players' backs or he'll be fighting nine, not five. Likewise, the spin doctors have to know the position of the other players, not only at the moment, but also later in the day, the week, the month. They know the players. They have no enemies—only friends on the other side. At the end of the day, they're all trying to split the same slice of pie.

To the casual observer, as well as to the doctrinaire purist, the spin doctors appear to have no principles. Critics deplore the fact that they often represent clients and interests at the opposite ends of the spectrum. But principles are a luxury they cannot afford. Their one abiding interest is in keeping the ecosystem thriving, in keeping its balance from tilting.

Their true enemies are those who do not see, understand, or value the interconnectedness of today's corporate business world—or those who are aware of this global industrial-commercial complex, but fear it and wish to destroy it. Those who are perfectly content, with only an occasional burst of righteous indignation, to let the spin doctors exercise their function vastly outnumber such critics. This occurs principally when they have either made the wrong decision (and thus lost money) or watched someone make more money than public opinion believes they are entitled to (the so-called obscene profits).

But no, the challenges faced by the spin doctors do not come from the naive, the purist, or the man in the street. They come from the change that they themselves set in motion.

CHALLENGES

Let's look at the analyst. He has become the sportswriter of Wall Street. We no longer look at the box scores and individual players' statistics; we simply read the sportswriters' commentary of the game. Baseball scouts don't rely on the sportswriters' colorful commentaries in making their individual player evaluations, but the corporate analyst has become, by the individual investor's default, the handicapper for The Street.

It is true that because of protections self-imposed by financial houses (such as the Chinese Wall, which keeps brokers from profiting from information in advance of the investing public), and other protections, the individual shareholder can generally rely on the analyst to perform as a fairly unbiased financial detective. But every investor should remember that while the analyst's only police-power words are buy, sell, or hold, these are truly power words. On any given day, billions of dollars in stock performance as well as the company executives' compensations ride on any one of them.

Today's challenge for the analyst lies in his very specialized focus on the stocks he tracks. He knows all those stocks intimately, but does he know the rest of the world? Is he ready for the BTU revolution? The analyst who has followed Hydrocarbon Man's stocks to the exclusion of other industries has to learn about BTU Man's universe. The best analyst in the world has a lot of work ahead of him. He and his peers have set forces loose that they need to control. They started the revolution, and their clients are on the front line. What marching orders do they give if they aren't familiar with the terrain? They set a new world in motion, but they need to retool before they can control their creation. The way they have always won is to write the rules of engagement. But remember the proverb, "He whom the gods want to destroy, they first give 40 years of success."

The spin doctors have maintained control of the corporate jungle over the years through their cunning, wit, and experience. They've made sure

119

their clients did not get fatally hurt or weakened, or take more than their fair share. Our Oklahoma sage likes to say (and practice) that old age and treachery will overcome youth and skill, but the jungle has changed. New and unfamiliar breeds have entered it. The smaller and more passive animals are more endangered than ever.

The magnitude of the dollars in the energy field is bringing in a new breed of nonindustry player. Technology advances give the less-prepared no place to hide. The spin doctors' greatest challenge will lie in the accelerating electricity deregulation that will occur during the next few years. The current quest for electricity traders with any hint of commodity trading knowledge is frantic. Knowledge of natural gas trading is preferred, but don't hesitate to apply with a working knowledge of interest rates, foreign currency, agriculture, metals–in short, any experience with futures and derivatives. They will teach you the power cash markets. Schedulers and dispatchers are in every bit as much demand as experienced offshore drilling personnel. Search firms are busy beyond their wildest imagination.

What will happen when the trader's disease suddenly comes out of remission? Who will be expected to have all of the experience and expertise to help all of their old friends manage this plethora of new tools and inexperienced talent? Why, the old reliable spin doctors, of course!

BIGGER BUCKS AND GENETIC DIVERSITY

One of the inherent weaknesses plaguing the BTU world is its enormity. For most BTU players, size becomes their very own worst enemy: The bigger you get, the bigger you *have* to get.

Majors cannot grow with stripper wells; they must go overseas or offshore to hunt for elephant fields in order to meet analysts' projections.

For investment bankers, due diligence for a small IPO costs as much as for a much larger one without the proportionately larger fees.

For consultants, a major oil or utility company means more fees than does a small start-up company.

Large law firms stay large as a result of large clients.

The world of the BTU spin doctors becomes an economy of scale.

It has been said that if there is too little genetic diversity, the species will die out. The same observation can certainly be made of corporations. To reiterate a point made earlier, spin doctors perform a very important and necessary function in the BTU world. However, a dangerous side effect that has emerged as a result of their size and interconnectedness is that everyone uses them. This dilemma, which probably arises out of defensive posturing as much as offensive strategizing, becomes a corporate Catch 22. Does a company use the same spin doctor as the competition so that, hopefully, neither company ends up with the competitive advantage? Or, does the company use a different spin doctor and dare to actually be different?

An example could be made with the airline industry. The executives have all come up through the same regulated/deregulated ranks and attended the same business schools, and they all retain the same spin doctors. The following question then arises. If you took the top five executives from the top ten airlines and shuffled them among those various ten airlines, could the investing public and travelers tell any significant difference?

Would the same be true in the BTU world? Probably.

When your think tanks become corporate love-ins, whom do they benefit? What happens to competitive differentiation?

A lot of the spin doctors are living off a very prosperous legacy. They have survived the test of time, but the accelerating energy revolution will be their biggest challenge yet. They will survive it, of course. Not only that, but they will master it. The question is, how many of their clients will?

The puppet masters need one hell of an opening act for the electric deregulation show. Of course, with this boomtown of activity and opportunity and this kind of money to be made, the promoter is sure to show up. What will he look like this time?

THE PROMOTER

"May he not be knave, fool and genius altogether?"
—Herman Melville, *The Confidence Man*

N o revolution is ever complete without a mercenary. Within the energy industry, the promoter has always excelled in this role. While promoters may not always understand revolutions and wars in general, the one thing they all understand exceedingly well are the spoils of war. Money gets their attention and keeps them coming back for more. It is the best way of keeping score that they know.

Like a good mercenary, a promoter possesses a certain siege mentality; his high energy level wears you down. He overflows. He takes over. He can't be contained. He can't be controlled. He can, however, be recognized.

Man, can he be recognized!

MAY THE FORCE BE WITH YOU

The promoter is one of the primal personality types on the planet. There are no shades, no tints, no tones to him; he is in the three primary colors, and you can see his aura most often before you see him. Experience allows one to sense his presence; as in *Star Wars,* "There is a disturbance in the force." Once you've entered his force field, it becomes very difficult to break out of it. Once you've let his excitement get you, what you probably cannot do, at least for a while, is leave his side.

You may not remember when he comes into your life; you'll never forget when he leaves it. He's always center stage, never behind the scenes. He's no spin doctor pulling strings, although there are usually spin doctors pulling his.

Nonetheless, standing alone, the promoter actually has many good, even admirable, traits. The only problem with the promoter is that he can't contain even himself. He is larger than life, and like life, he just *is*. Like life, he's what happens to you while you're attempting to make other plans.

THE CONCEPT OF LEMONADE

There are only two kinds of promoters—the good promoter, and the bad promoter. The good promoter makes you money; the bad promoter loses you money. There aren't any other kinds of promoters. A mediocre promoter is a contradiction in terms.

A promoter is always on one side of the scale or the other; he's never in the middle. A balanced promoter is a salesman. A salesman believes in the product; a promoter believes in the sale. A salesman has to have a product; all a promoter needs is a concept. A promoter is someone who has no lemons, no container, no cups, and no ice but has a sign up that reads, "Lemonade—25 cents a glass."

Promoters have their favorite tried-and-tested tricks of the trade. For instance, when showing a geological prospect, a good promoter will go to great lengths to insure that his presentation intentionally leaves out some key element, such as a very noticeable dry hole next to his prospect. When asked about the significance of the dry hole, the chagrined presenter always thanks the mullet profusely for bringing such an important omission to his immediate attention.

Why, that dry hole had such sizeable showings in the Red Fork formation that it set up this particular rare geological opportunity, and he had forgotten to even mention it! Unfortunately, the poor operator who drilled that well 40 years ago was looking for the Arbuckle and didn't have our current technology to capitalize on a tight sand formation such as this. With the analytical and completion tools now available, this passed-over opportunity now looks like the same company-maker that Joe Bob recently found 10 miles down the road. *We* can't miss, can we?

So, after the mullet has ingeniously found the dry hole with impressive Red Fork shows, how can they *not* have a big discovery on their hands?

Since this is now *his* prospect too, of course the mullet would love to have the opportunity to be a part of a quality prospect such as this.

Bass fishing with live bait was never this easy.

THE NEW BREED OF ROBBER BARONS

Most true oilies would share this confession—one they can never really discuss freely with their cronies at the Petroleum Club or at other industry functions, that they truly miss J.R. Ewing!

Not only do they miss him—they all want him back. He made things happen, and he did so with great flair.

His deals always got done and his wells didn't just come in—they came in big. Some people live well, but J.R. lived exceedingly well. He seemed to have coined the phrase, "Living well is the best revenge." Private jets, fast cars, sleek horses, and, of course, beautiful women. No wonder everyone loved to hate him—everyone was green with envy.

While everyone condemned his ethics and lifestyle in public, they all wanted in on all of his deals. They all hit big! After all, Cliff and Digger Barnes were there to drill dry holes on all the leases J.R. had picked over! They all wanted to be invited to his parties because that was where all of the beautiful women were. J.R. may have created negative images, but he also created positive cash flows. Ewing Oil surely employed lots of people. J.R. may have been an arrogant jerk, but operating a drilling rig for him as an industry professional was a much-preferred alternative to operating the sour-cream gun on the Taco Bell assembly line.

Back in the '70s and early '80s, every oilie knew at least one J.R.—handsome, smooth-talking, irresistible, confident, and, by all appearances, very successful...the promoter.

Blue Skies and Sunshine

You've heard of the Blue Sky Laws–those laws that protect investors from unscrupulous promoters. How aptly named! It is always very difficult to think of anything but blue skies and happy thoughts when a true promoter is around. Failure, hard times, and unhappy investors and creditors always seem so remote and unlikely when the promoter is singing his song.

Kind of funny how all of those things disappear so quickly the minute he slips into the shadows.

While the true promoter always personifies excitement and enthusiasm, he guards against feeling true emotion. This is not a problem. He is emotionally unavailable. Remember Gordon Gekko's advice to young Bud Fox in *Wall Street*? "Never get emotional over money."

Fear, ego, and greed drive all markets, as we saw in earlier chapters, but the promoter strives to mask his own symptoms of this trio of emotions. However, he most often serves as the disease's deadly carrier, causing flagrant reactions in others. As swamps serve as fertile breeding grounds for mosquitoes, the oil patch has always been a fertile breeding ground for promoters. In springtime in Oklahoma, you never get used to the incessant howl of sirens announcing threatening weather detected by Doppler radar systems. Wouldn't it be useful to have an advance warning system for unusual and threatening promoter activity?

What's in a Name–Tornado or Twister?

Someone once mused, if you think it's hard to get into the good ol' boys club, wait until you try to get out.

True enough, once you're in the fraternal club, everyone wants to help you, and too many good deals–just like too much good food and liquor–can eventually do you in. Ironically, the clubbishness and the brotherhood are helped along by the Southwest's affinity for initials or double names. No known reason, that's just the way it is. J.R., J.C., Joe Bob, Billy Bob, Jim Bob. Even the women are Ada Marie, Nancy Lou, Betty Sue. Can't explain that one either. Then we have the initial-name combos–T. Boone, J. Frank, or J. Clifford.

Okay, what's in a name, you say?

Come on, how can you not trust a guy named Billy Bob? You just never really think that a Joe Bob could get into your wallet very deep without you knowing and very purposefully looking the other way. Besides, who wants to drill a well with someone named William Robert?

And how about Thelma Lou? She sounds like someone your father took to the senior prom. How in the world could you not trust someone your own father would date?

Well, then what's the difference between a tornado and a divorce from Thelma Lou? Nothing–either way you lose your trailer home. Maybe it's just those Southwestern handles. Who knows? One day your best friend–the next day your co-defendant.

WILL THE REAL PROMOTER PLEASE STAND UP?

Okay, so we all agree that promoters possess strong social skills, high risk-tolerance, irrepressibility, an impeccable sense of timing, and a very strong desire for the expensive things in life–as in the old Penn Square toast, "Here's to beautiful horses, fast women, and old whiskey."

Most promoters don't have any real technological know-how *per se,* but that doesn't matter because they know how to sell the concept–*any* concept–extremely well.

While promoters have an instant appreciation for objects of value, either present or future, they rarely allow themselves to develop any emotional attachment to them. This differentiates them from many producers, who become slaves to their prospects, just as farmers become emotional slaves to their land.

Promoters always go to the opportunity; the commodity itself is of no consequence to this personality type, whether it is oil and gas, real estate, securities, etc. So the promoter leaves the energy community in the downturns and returns in the upswings. One obsession merely replaces another. He has a gifted and uncanny sixth sense of money flows.

Promoters always think of themselves as fairly honest individuals. They never lie. They always tell the truth, even if they have to make it up. If their incurable enthusiasm forces them to tell some variation of the truth, they usually only do so in the hope of achieving a better or more convenient truth than previously existed. If caught in the act of misrepresenting the truth, they become sincerely offended-not because they were caught in the act, but because their efforts in trying to create a better and happier truth went unappreciated. They may occasionally suffer a bruised ego, but they never allow themselves to become a bruised optimist.

Chutzpah is a good word to describe promoters–as in the story of the young man who shoots both of his parents and then throws himself on the mercy of the court because he's an orphan. If promoters are under attack, they're hurt, not because you're on to them, but because their urge to do good has been misunderstood as potentially self-serving.

They are always civic-minded for as long as they are in town and the game is afoot. The promoter completely understands and accepts the fact that being broke is a temporary condition and that being poor is an unacceptable state of mind. To a promoter, success is a mind game–today, tomorrow, and forever.

SWEET DREAMS AND TIME MACHINES

What always lets them back in the door are prices, no matter what the catalyst for prices may be at any given moment. All the promoter ever needs is a good story and an audience. God only knows how badly the financial community and the investors always need and want a good story. In the late '70s the *raison d'être* was national security, today its 3-D seismic and technology.

A very revealing promoter story concerns the opportunist from Washington D.C. who was promoting oil ventures in west Texas. His spiel went something like this: "I've got this time machine that will take you back millions of years and present you with a gift that God put there just for you." A lesser talent would have spoken of a drilling rig that would cut through geological time periods to the prospective formation to find oil, if you signed on the dotted line, and gave him a check.

Remember the story of the young businessman who had money but no experience? He met a promoter who had experience but didn't have any money. Now the promoter has all of the money and the young businessman has all of the experience. More often than not, the best wood in a promoter's golf bag is his pencil.

We're talking about revolutions here and promoters make very good revolutionaries. They are particularly keen at exciting crowds into action and then advancing to the rear before the bullets begin to fly. The blood of fallen comrades gives them great courage, although the sight of their own makes them faint.

The general public may have very little personal contact with the J.R.s of the BTU world, but a close examination of the balance sheets of the energy companies they deal with may provide great insight as to their presence.

SNAKE CHARMERS

Institutions and people change, societal needs alter the way the energy world functions, technological advances let us all leap forward, but certain personality traits will always dominate other personality traits.

Promoters are typically very creative and imaginative people. They see an opportunity and create a market to complement it. It's not so much that they are totally rogue individuals, it's more that they are opportunists. Because they see the opportunity first, they are often in the midst of the deal before there are any real ground rules. Much of the blame and accusations directed at them stems from jealousy and anger at having been beaten to a lucrative market in one's very own backyard.

We might just as well enjoy the colorful tapestry these strong individuals weave, because no constraint–regulatory, corporate, or otherwise–will ever totally, successfully rein them in. Historically, we have only been able to respond after the fact. In other words, we only close the barn door after the horse is out and gone. The only real, effective safeguard and prevention over the years has been maturity and experience.

But with the current generation skip, can the young cadre catch them or fully comprehend their tricks of the trade? A ranch dog that survives his first rattlesnake strike becomes a dangerous adversary at all future reptile encounters.

SECTION V: THE DESTINATION

It's 2001

"Coming events cast their shadow."

—Anonymous

"The future was predictable, but hardly anyone predicted it."

—Allen Kay

Napoleon once said, "History is a fable told by the victors."
So who's going to get to write this particular fable? Who's going
to end up winning this power play?

Revolutions are named by historians looking backward, not by
the revolutionaries looking forward. The revolutionaries are generally too
busy with the war and too focused on the final score to be thinking up historical names.

When Luther hammered his protests to his cathedral's door, he
didn't stand there and shout, "This will be known as the Reformation!"

When the Luddites destroyed machinery, the machines' owners did
not scold them for impeding the Industrial Revolution. They destroyed the
Luddites because they had destroyed the masters' private property; the handle came later.

However, there is one activity that revolutionaries always find
enough time to engage in. That activity is to come up with ringing slogans
and galvanizing mottoes. (Keep repeating to yourself: "Show me a great revolutionary and I'll show you a great marketer/promoter.")

The ongoing revolution has certainly had those who have fought the
regulation of what used to be viewed as natural monopolies so they could
get into the money game. Their slogans make no mention of that. Instead,
the revolutionaries have raised the banner of deregulation and multiple pennants hailing all its virtues to come.

We have seen how deregulation has been glorified and its consequences endowed with unassailable value. The revolutionaries of the last
quarter of the twentieth century have not discussed any of the issues you
have been reading throughout this book. In fact, those issues have been very
carefully buried.

But surely by the end of the twentieth century, we know for an
absolute fact that the law of unintended consequences works with no less
infallible accuracy than the laws of thermodynamics. And we have seen how
unintended consequences have come to trip up many of the golden benefits
touted by the deregulation warriors.

Yes, the deregulation revolutionaries have won their wars so far. But
have America's consumers?

When the winning side's historians write their final critique, will
they call this the Energy Revolution?

What would they call it if they were writing that critique
today—before BTU Man wakes up to the opportunity he *still* has of controlling the process and getting his, and the country's, needs met?

Historians ought to at least subtitle it, "The People's Default." On the
other hand, if BTU Man starts controlling the process, the subtitle might well
be, "Power to the People."

To best understand past and current events, they must be viewed
from the perspective of those experiencing them rather than from the van-
tage point of those writing about them.

A reshaping of the energy world has been not only inevitable, but
also necessary. The deregulation of the natural gas industry was long in coming, and its results have by and large been beneficial. The reshaping of the
electric industry is not only inevitable, but also necessary.

It is the *execution* of that reshaping that is in question.

Whose power play is this, anyway?

BTU MAN, IT'S HAPPENING TO Y-O-U

Few industries have produced such a variety of colorful characters in such a short time as the energy industry. We have seen and endured–and are still seeing and enduring–the robber barons, the wildcatters, the promoters, the regulators, and the spin doctors.

Just as the tobacco companies, with Joe Camel and the Marlboro Man, addicted a gullible public, so the energy players and their masters addicted Hydrocarbon Man to petroleum products to the point of inelasticity. He has to have the products regardless of their costs. Already, in 1958, economist John Kenneth Galbraith noted, "In the affluent society, no useful distinction can be made between luxuries and necessaries."

The passing of the baton should be interesting, to say the least. Now the Time Bandits are coming after you and your wallet. You can run, BTU Man, but you can't hide. There will be no escape from the onslaught. It will include your mail, telephone, TV, radio, Internet, billboards, newspapers, and magazines. Their expectation of achieving a better or more convenient truth than previously existed relies on your continued inattention.

Algebra teaches us to solve for the unknown. In the energy business, the unknown will always be the mullet. If you can figure out ahead of time who the mullet is going to be, you can then conclude who has the greatest stake in his welfare at that particular moment–and that's who is going to end up with the prize.

The stranded-investment issue explored in Chapter 2 is illustrative of the smoke and mirrors that always exist when large sums of money are at stake.

There's always got to be a game in town; without a game, without motion, the implication is that we have economic stagnation. The truth is that those outside a monopoly lack access to the money machine. They have no currency. To get at it, they have to convince the mass audience that a change will be of enormous benefit to *everybody*. After the currency seekers have gotten hold of the money-making machine, the mass audience finds

137

out who is going to be paying the entry fee, maintenance assessments and exit fee. The mass audience is.

The money machine needs constant reengineering. For example, when a peer has been left out of the game and threatens an outcry, it's more prudent to let him in than it is to defend one's turf. That makes the pie smaller, so it's necessary to kick somebody out of the game. You want a realist's definition of the one that gets tagged? It's somebody with some level of responsibility that was present but having too much fun counting the money he thought he was going to make to be paying much attention. The one who wrote the check but didn't bother to read the rule book.

Remember that just because a person has money doesn't mean that person understands the game.

A wave of reengineering becomes necessary after deregulation has been in effect for a while. Newcomers–many of them the usual mullets–have flocked into the market, having bought into the lure of open competition as promised by the revolutionaries. But the last thing the revolutionaries truly want is a level playing field; they want only the *illusion* of competition. So after the newcomers have been lured into the game–and after their dues have been collected–the power play begins.

By this time most of them have lost their enthusiasm, their sense of humor, and possibly their opportunity capital, as the profit margin in an overcrowded market has become entirely too thin for their resources. Some of them, however, have researched customer needs well enough to create a valuable niche. As a result, they have developed staying power. They look solid enough to stay and to possibly even become a threat to the established revolutionaries.

These people have to go.

The longer the game lasts–the longer the more alert participants have to figure out the niches and the loopholes–the more level the playing field becomes. It's time for the revolutionaries to reengineer the rules–perhaps reevaluating that old-fashioned antitrust legislation–so they can concentrate on their next power grab.

Isn't it true that when you walk into a crowded function, you just assume that everybody has been there a long time and knows what's going on? That allows everyone present to be able to say, "I just got here." That's what spin doctors call *plausible deniability*. That's what Sharon Stone in *Basic Instinct* called "suspension of disbelief."

Everybody has a dog in this fight. No pickpocket works alone; commotion has to be created. Whoever is pointing the finger at the victim is the likely pickpocket.

THE SHAPE OF CHANGE

Throughout time, the energy industry has been reluctant to change, yet change has been the only constant for this most global of all industries.

Today, the industry is on the verge of the most important structural change in its history. Causes and effects ripple up and down the BTU value stream. Mergers, acquisitions, divestitures, and restructuring are the order of the day.

Worldwide demand for crude oil and its products is growing at an alarming rate and shows no sign of abating as Third World countries improve their economic output and standards of living. BTU Man will face more and more global competition for all of the products he has become so accustomed to having readily available at very affordable prices. Not only BTU Man, but the energy participants and those charged with determining and guiding energy policy, will face a formidable task: How to ensure the continuation of available and affordable energy.

Companies must go beyond their traditional thinking to parlay their core competencies and industry experience into tangible, marketable assets. The existing infrastructure feels the demands on its system growing by the day. Both shareholders and their competition are seriously challenging corporations and their management. They no longer have the luxury of sitting on the sidelines waiting for the markets to emerge. Will they transform their organizations–and by doing so set industry standards–or will they be content to follow the farsighted few?

Will we have crisis- and competitor-led transformation or foresight-led transformation?

In the world of competition, companies must prepare to be a better enemy.

As we look back across the BTU value stream, we see an industry that is increasingly being led and dominated by companies seeking to achieve total integration.

These companies, just like the major oil companies, will be involved in supply chains that will run from the wellhead to the burnertip. As these companies continue the integration cycle into the power sector, the supply chain will go through the complete metamorphosis from the hydrocarbon at the wellhead to the electron at the electrical outlet. This integration becomes necessary as companies recognize that price volatility and increased competition will continue to cause close scrutiny of their balance sheets by analysts. One sector's revenue becomes another sector's cost.

Today, integration is an example of preparation meeting opportunity. Looking not just down the BTU value stream, but to other global commodity industries such as agriculture and metals, you will find dominance lies in the hands of similarly integrated companies. Energy, as with all other commodities, must have favorable prices to attract and sustain the interest of capital markets. And these markets will be increasingly intolerant of boom-and-bust cycles.

Another strong indicator of the growth of integration in the industry is the emergence of gas utilities in the E&P sector.

David W. Wilson, principal, strategic and advisory services at Coopers & Lybrand L.L.P., states the integration case.

"We know of numerous utilities that have become involved in E&P either directly or through financing of producing or developmental properties, and this trend is growing. There are many reasons for this interest. First, many utilities have significant cash flows from their regulated assets, with few opportunities to reinvest in regulated assets at attractive rates.

"Second, they are already in the gas business and particularly understand the market and transportation sectors. They see the value of integration and are spending money to build their value-added strategy. They believe that they can earn a superior return in E&P if they bring some of their risk-management and marketing capabilities to the process."

Oh–and the wildcatter of the future?

You remember that devil-may-care, one-roll-of-the-dice, risk-it-all oil man. He's probably going to look a lot different. Wilson, through his

Houston-based Energy Strategic and Advisory Services Group, believes that he knows the wildcatters of the future.

"They will be from utilities and financial institutions and will be more familiar with Black Scholes option models than oil and gas economic programs. They will be looking for opportunities that will allow them to be players in E&P without enduring the inevitable boom-and-bust cycles. They will be very concerned with the net income effects on their companies. They will talk about balancing their portfolios. They will use price forecasts based on the financial markets, and they won't buy into projects in the anticipation of large price increases.

"They will be willing to buy expertise they don't feel that they have, but will not be willing to just write checks and turn the program over to companies as they have in the past. They will be more interested in looking at past track records and histories of reserves successes than in learning about down-thrown faults and by-passed producers. In short, the wildcatters of the future will be more financially oriented than geologists or engineers. They will probably pick up the *Wall Street Journal* before the morning drilling report."

If politics makes for strange bedfellows, you ain't seen nothin' yet. The BTU value stream is going to look like summertime barge traffic on the Mississippi River. Producers are going to be rafting downstream looking for partners while utilities will be paddling their way upstream looking for reserves to complete their integration objectives. The Bible's peaceful truce between the lion and the lamb will pale in comparison to some of the joint ventures between small independents and major oil companies.

Analysts are going to be sitting on the banks watching with keen interest as the investment bankers cruising on their yachts toss out life preservers. Ol' J.R. and all kinds of other privateers will have a glorious time fighting over control of the SoSueMe Yacht Club. And oh, by the way, look for T. Boone to come out of the shadows for this maritime three-ring circus.

Perhaps an issue where change will make an enormous impact is that of *orphan investments*.

They will emerge when the dust settles, after all of the mega-mergers are finally approved and completed. After all, even when change is fully expected, it is very difficult to prepare for. When the *jumbo combos* finally get around to evaluating all of their merged assets, there will be a collection of assets that will be either redundant or incapable of efficiently merging into the new corporate entity. These will be the *orphan assets*.

They will still have value to the right entity, just not to the *jumbo combos*. This class of assets will be very similar to the U.S. oil properties the major oil companies sold to the independents. They bought them because they can produce and operate them more economically than can the majors. The orphan assets will create a significant payday for the lawyers, investment bankers, and consultants among the spin doctors. The analysts among them, already familiar with most of these assets, will have a field day reworking them into the acquiring companies' balance sheets.

A New Set of Hands

As energy deregulation meets free-market forces in a world being constantly remade through innovation and technology, unprecedented change results—and at a pace that is almost impossible to recognize, interpret, or control.

The *acceleration* of change may prove to be very difficult to measure.

Against this chaotic backdrop, the energy revolution has been shifting the controls of its enormous profit engine away from traditional hands to a new set of hands. Because whoever controls energy has the potential to control society, the issue of controls is paramount.

The mass consumer, who has paid little to no attention to deregulation of any kind—past, present and future—needs to wake up and focus on a scary fact. The stakes get higher every time he ignores the changes created when monopolies give way to free markets. BTU Man must now earn his self-anointed title of master of the universe by facing and making some very difficult decisions. He can no longer drive to a Save Mother Earth protest in a gas-guzzling Chevy Suburban. He must realize that while it's his responsibility to save the endangered whale, he must allow for additional exploration to permit the dinosaur's legacy to continue.

Energy is the biggest marketing game the American consumer has ever seen. It's the biggest deregulation the Baby Boomers have witnessed and the very first for Generation X.

Generations aside, every person who consumes energy, votes, or invests, or who has an environmental concern or a retirement plan is interconnected with the accelerating BTU revolution. Decisions have been and continue to be made that create an impact greater than ever before on all Americans' lives and futures. Americans need to know what indifference will cost them, their communities, and their children.

There are those who ask, "What is the call to arms? The market's higher than it's ever been, the American lifestyle is at an absolute zenith. So who are you calling complacent? In brief, why are you asking me to study repair manuals for something that ain't broke yet?"

The answer is equally brief. Murphy's Law of Unintended Consequences dictates that it will break only at the most inopportune time and at the greatest cost and inconvenience possible.

(Then there are those who ask, along with Groucho Marx, "What has posterity ever done for me?")

Who will exercise the controls necessary to keep a $300-billion industry operating on a truly level playing field?

Energy is too basic to the life of all consumers for them to continue ignoring the people responsible for providing it. Consumers must start taking an intelligently responsible interest in understanding this breed of people–their origins, their opportunities and risks, their evolution, their migration path–as they learn how to create and maintain market share in the enormous market playing out before them, in the industry whose future they guide. Energy is not something that is provided by the evil ones. Energy players are not the profit-crazed enemies of the consumer portrayed by some groups. It's high time the consumers stopped viewing their relationship with the energy industry as a necessarily adversarial process.

Rather than remain idle bystanders and/or negative critics, consumers can participate. They can leverage, rather than merely accept. They too can get into the money machine.

Why leave it all for the revolutionaries to enjoy?

The final deregulation of energy is becoming a reality. The dinosaur is running free once more. Tremendous wealth is going to be created and transferred. The revolution was fought in your name, BTU Man. It's only fit-

143

ting that you should be a beneficiary. You've been on a journey. Now you understand the game and the players. Pick your side wisely.

The consumer isn't the only one who needs to alter his pattern of action or inaction. It's high time that energy players took the trouble to understand their customers and acknowledge that the commodity is the vehicle that drives them to the market. By and large, energy players have focused on what they know how to do best and on force-feeding the consumer the product *du jour*. Now they are faced with offering products that are still evolving to customers who are starting to order off the menu.

Will consumers and energy players learn to communicate their needs and wants in an increasingly transparent market?

The hostile relationship grew out of two circumstances. First, the historical villains such as John D. Rockefeller and other Robber Barons and the Hollywood- and TV-created fictional characters; second, energy buyer and seller have traditionally not met face to face. In a rigidly regulated industry, the consumer's opinions and desires are almost irrelevant to the product or service. A deregulated industry, however, is ideally characterized by market transparency. That's what is really meant by free markets.

With today's lifting of the regulatory, monopoly veil, energy buyers and sellers will have the opportunity to explore their needs in a nonadversarial relationship. It is only from this bilateral discovery process that the product and the market will truly evolve.

Alvin Toffler described "change" as the process by which the future invades our lives and "future shock" as the stress and disorientation caused by too much change in too short a time. The energy revolution is unquestionably causing a lot of change very fast, and it is human nature to shelve the whole matter and hope it sorts itself out.

But it won't. The critical question for BTU Man to answer and act on is, "How will he keep up with the incessant demand for change that will characterize his new world?"

Will he wake up in time to exercise controls on the energy deregulation process so that it answers his–and North America's–needs?

Or will he become a victim of the greatest power play of all time?

APPENDICES

APPENDIX I: THE BARREL

There are 42 U.S. gallons in a barrel of crude, or 35 King's (later Imperial) gallons. This measurement officially dates back to 1482, to the reign of King Edward IV of England. It was decided to put an end to rampantly deceitful trading practices in the herring trade by establishing the barrel holding 35 King's gallons as the standard size for packing herring. At the time of this royal decree, herring fishing was the largest trade industry in the North Sea; today it's crude oil.

But did the King's Barrel measurement originate with herring, or was it a measurement already in use that was conveniently extended to herring?

Did the measurement come into being to store the product of another ocean denizen? How about whale oil?

Whaling by Europeans–first from land, and eventually in Atlantic waters–is said to have first been pursued by the Basques, possibly as early as the tenth century. The Dutch and then the British joined the Basques in the hunt, in what became a business of large profits.

Transplanted to the American colonies, whaling launched the economic expansion of New England. By the early 1700s, the whale of choice was the sperm whale, whose head holds as much as a ton of the finest oil then available for illumination. By 1790, the standard container of illuminating oil was codified as the barrel of 35 King's gallons.

Whaling declined in the 1850s, and then, Colonel Drake drilled the first producing oil well in the United States near Titusville, Pennsylvania, in August 1859. In those early, feverish, times oil men and traders kept crude in any kind of handy barrel. Coopers finally began making barrels especially for crude oil and by 1866 Pennsylvania producers had formally adopted the 42-gallon barrel as their standard. And of course the principal use of that early crude was to make kerosene–for illumination.

Funny how fish stories turn out.

WHAT'S IN A BARREL?

Before crude oil can be consumed in its final form, such as gasoline or diesel, it must be refined. This is a process of cooking and distilling that actually turns the 42 gallons of crude into a little more than 44 gallons of petroleum products. The 2+ gallons appear through molecular shifting, or a rearranging of the molecules–a refining term known as the processing gain.

Refining is done in stages. The first step occurs as crude oil is heated at the bottom of a distillation tower. The oil turns to gas and rises, with various portions of the barrel contents condensing into liquids at different heights of the tower. What's left over at the bottom is then put through a similar tower that has a vacuum at the top. This process takes out the portions of the oil too heavy to be collected the first time through.

Crude oils range from light sweet, the most desirable blend, to heavy sour, the least desirable. What's meant by a crude oil's "sweetness" is the measure of its sulfur content.

Statistics from the U.S. Department of Energy's Energy Information Administration show that when the refining is done, a little less than half of the barrel (19.50 gallons) has been converted into finished motor gasoline.

The other products from a barrel include distillate fuel oil, 8.61 gallons; jet fuel, 4.20 gallons; residual fuel oil, 2.77 gallons; petroleum coke, 1.60 gallons; asphalt and road oil, 1.39 gallons; liquefied gases, 1.43 gallons; petrochemical feedstocks, 1.22 gallons; kerosene, 0.25 gallon; finished aviation gasoline, 0.08 gallon; and miscellaneous products, 2.98 gallons.

APPENDIX II: THE MCF

For openers, natural gas is measured in cubic feet, typically in units of 1,000 cubic feet. This is written as Mcf. One million cubic feet is written as MMcf; one billion as Bcf; one trillion as Tcf.

How does that Mcf get into the marketing stream?

The chain starts with natural gas accumulations in the depths of the planet, predominantly the result of eons of decomposition of various organisms through heat and pressure. These accumulations are in porous and permeable beds of so-called reservoir rock–usually limestone, sandstone, or dolomite. The gas is kept from slithering out of its bed by a trap–an impermeable cap rock, usually shale.

Natural gas deposits either keep company with crude oil deposits, or keep to themselves. It's called associated gas when found with crude oil deposits, and all the oilfields in the world hold significant amounts of associated gas. Typically, crude oil and its associated gas are trapped in relatively young rocks at depths above 12,000 feet.

When natural gas is found in deposits containing relatively insignificant quantities of crude, it's called non-associated gas. Most of the world's largest gas fields hold non-associated gas and are at depths far below those of most oilfields. Non-associated gas has been found in commercial quantities in rocks up to 600 million years old, and to a depth of 31,441 feet.

So, the chain leads the gas out of the ground, into the pipeline, and onto the market—right?

Well, not exactly.

Associated gas does not always make it out of the ground. Crude oil frequently needs so-called artificial lift, in the form of a pumping mechanism, to flow to the surface. The decision can be made to reinject the associated gas into the reservoir for increased pressurization (leading to greater oil recovery and longer reservoir life).

Even if reinjection is not necessary, associated gas may still not be produced. If gas is flooding the markets, or a gas distribution system is lacking, then flaring (burning off the gas at the production site) often follows, especially outside the United States.

Non-associated gas generally flows from its reservoir without assistance, but again, if production is economically undesirable, the well may be temporarily shut in, pending a more favorable gas market. (Trouble is, in some cases this causes reservoir damage and a permanently impaired flow rate, leaving the producer with a Catch-22 situation.)

And, as we had to do with crude oil, we have to look at the composition of natural gas, which varies from field to field.

While methane and other light hydrocarbons are usually the major components, varying proportions of other materials are found also–and none of these are accepted into a sales pipeline without a trip through the gas processing plant. Take plain ol' water. In liquid or vapor form, water is always present in reservoirs; if it isn't removed from the gas, it leads to pipeline corrosion and/or plugging of equipment.

The first step toward the processing plant is the gathering system. Gathering lines–generally 2 to 6 inches in diameter but sometimes up to 36 inches–carry the gas over what is typically a short distance from the wellheads.

But wait! There's a detour. First comes the compression station. Natural gas expands hugely once it is brought to the atmospheric pressure of the earth's surface. Fortunately, unlike crude oil, natural gas is highly compressible, so that when it exits the compression station, it's compressed to 700 pounds/square inch (psi)–1,000 Mcf is compressed down to about 20 Mcf of volume.

Now we're in the processing plant. It takes the raw natural gas from the wellhead and prepares it for sale in two ways:

• It reduces or removes undesirable components, such as carbon dioxide and hydrogen sulfide, known as sour gas. Both are corrosive gases and, in the latter's case, poisonous.

• The plant extracts the natural gas liquids (NGLs) from the natural gas stream.

These NGLs are nonmethane hydrocarbons that are typically further processed at a so-called fractionation plant into commercially desirable products such as ethane; propane and butane, to be marketed as liquefied petroleum gas (LPG); and condensates, for use in refineries, as chemical feedstock, or directly as fuel.

And because purified natural gas is odorless and colorless, a final safety-measure process adds sulfur-containing compounds called *mercaptans*, whose strong odor makes it possible to detect a gas leak.

Finally, it's ready for the sales (transmission) pipeline.

Because each of these pipelines has slightly different requirements, there is no one listing of what constitutes this pipeline-quality product. In all likelihood, its methane content hovers around 90%, ethane around 6%, and oxygen and propane may be at 2%, with minute quantities of water vapor content, carbon dioxide, and hydrogen sulfide.

A Virginia gunsmith who was drilling a water well strung the first natural gas pipeline together in 1821. Aaron Hart, the story goes, heard a hissing sound, and realized his water well had gas in it. He is credited with drilling the first natural gas well on the continent. With commendable ingenuity, he piped the gas through hollowed logs to light and heat nearby buildings.

(A more complete description is to be found in *Fundamentals of Petroleum, 3rd Edition*, Mildred Gerding, editor, the University of Texas at Austin, 1986.)

Progress in pipeline construction proved excruciatingly slow, with concomitantly high delivery costs (hence, the oil man's traditional view of striking gas as a curse). Finally, technological advances at the end of World War II led to natural gas transmission lines of significant scale.

However, it was the federal deregulation of natural gas–culminating in the FERC's 1992's Order 636–that, by granting the fuel economic independence and value, led to the leaping growth in the natural gas pipeline network throughout the North American continent.

Pipelines today represent long-distance, high-pressure, high-volume transportation. Pipe diameter is up to 56 inches, and operating pressures are reaching beyond 1,000 psi.

(Not all natural gas is shipped via pipeline. Natural gas can be turned into liquefied natural gas (LNG) by lowering its temperature to -260°. LNG, which takes up approximately 16 times less storage space than natural gas, travels on the high seas in specialized cigar-shaped tankers. Once at its destination, the liquid fuel regains its gaseous form simply by having its temperature raised.)

Now that natural gas is a deregulated product, it has become a highly volatile commodity subject to the law of supply and demand. And the latter's wide swings call for the use of storage facilities, which commonly employ subsurface features such as depleted gas fields or salt-dome caverns. Customers use storage services to even out purchases or sales of natural gas throughout the year. Storage services play a critical role in the peak-period deliverability process of a great number of interstate natural gas pipelines and distributors.

APPENDIX III: THE ELECTRON

The electric power industry, at the dawn of deregulation, stands as one of the largest industries in the United States.

At the end of 1996, it boasted revenues of $200 billion and assets of $500 billion. There were a total of 3,050 electric utilities, including 1,971 public/municipal companies; 881 rural cooperatives; 192 investor-owned utilities (IOUs), and 6 federal companies (such as the Tennessee Valley Authority).

The IOUs controlled 76% of the country's generating capacity, 14% was in the hands of the municipals, 8% was with the co-ops, and 2% was with the federal entities.

The electric industry has three primary functions: generation, transmission, and distribution.

Unlike the coast-to-coast natural gas pipeline network, the electricity transmission grid is divided into four sections—Western, Eastern, ERCOT, and Quebec. The electric utilities and power pools manage these networks, matching generation with demand on a minute-to-minute basis.

The North American Electric Reliability Council (NERC) was formed in 1968 in the aftermath of the November 9, 1965, blackout that affected the northeastern United States and Ontario, Canada. NERC's mission is to promote the reliability of the electricity supply for North America. In short, NERC helps electric utilities and other electricity suppliers work together to keep the power flowing.

The membership of NERC is unique. It is a not-for-profit corporation whose owners are ten regional councils, one of whom is an affiliate council. The members of these regional councils come from all segments of the electricity supply industry—investor-owned utilities; federal, state, municipal, and provincial utilities; rural electric cooperatives; independent power producers; power marketers, and electricity brokers.

These entities account for virtually all of the electricity supplied in the United States, Canada, and a portion of the Baja California Norte, Mexico.

The NERC Regions are as follows:
- East Central Area Reliability Coordination Agreement (ECAR)
- Electric Reliability Council of Texas (ERCOT)
- Mid-Atlantic Area Council (MAAC)
- Mid-America Interconnected Network (MAIN)
- Mid-Continent Area Power Pool (MAPP)
- Northeast Power Coordinating Council (NPCC)
- Southeastern Electric Reliability Council (SERC)
- Southwest Power Pool (SPP)
- Western Systems Coordinating Council (WSCC)
  `The affiliate member is the Alaskan System Coordination Council.

A power pool is an association of two or more interconnected electric systems that agree to coordinate operations and planning for improved reliability and efficiencies, such as WSPP, SPP, NEPool, etc.

Congress established five federal power marketing administrations (PMAs) to sell hydroelectric power generated by federal dams and power plants. These PMAs and their headquarters follow:
- Alaska Power Administration (APA)–Juneau, Alaska
- Bonneville Power Administration (BPA)–Portland, Oregon
- Southeastern Power Administration (SEPA)–Elberton, Georgia
- Southwestern Power Administration (SWPA)–Tulsa, Oklahoma
- Western Area Power Administration (WAPA)–Golden, Colorado

The Tennessee Valley Authority (TVA) is a separately constituted federal power agency that serves similar functions and customers. Its headquarters are in Chattanooga, Tennessee.

APPENDIX IV: THE BASIS

Among the most important energy-trading relationships to understand is the ever-changing one between energy physical prices and the futures exchanges prices that is known as the *basis* or *basis differential*.

Basis is the amount that the local physical price is above or below the current price of the nearest futures delivery month, or *spot month*.

Differences in location–or more specifically, differences in transportation cost between locations–are certainly the major reasons that energy prices differ from one location to the other. Remember that price differences between specific locations are subject to change. Major supply-demand and transportation developments that affect futures prices usually have a similar impact on local physical prices. Sudden local shifts in supply and demand or transportation can distort this relationship temporarily, causing basis fluctuations.

Physical and futures prices usually move up and down in tandem–but not always. Nor do they often move in the exact same amount. Every local energy market is different and subject to many variables. It is important to understand that, while a futures market hedges an approximate physical position, the dynamics of the local physical market can't be ignored. Yesterday's location disadvantage can become tomorrow's location advantage.

So it's very important to understand that changes in basis can cause significant changes in expected profit-loss opportunities.

BASIS PRINCIPLES

Basis terminology can be very confusing at times, even for seasoned trading veterans. If basis is defined as the physical price minus the futures price, then basis weakens when

- the futures price rises more than the physical price
- the futures price declines less than the physical price
- the futures price rises while the physical price declines

CRUDE OIL EXAMPLE

Physicals	Futures		Basis
Day 1	$19.00	$20.00	($1.00)
Day 30	$18.50	$19.75	($1.25)

Basis weakened by $0.25 per barrel.

Basis strengthens when
- the futures price declines more than the physical price
- the futures price rises less than the physical price
- the futures price declines while the physical price rises

UNLEADED GASOLINE EXAMPLE

Physicals	Futures		Basis
Day 1	$0.5500	$0.7500	($0.2000)
Day 30	$0.7500	$0.8500	($0.1000)

Basis strengthened by $0.1000 per gallon.

In other words, the more positive the basis, the greater the strength of the local physical price in relation to the futures exchange. Conversely, the more negative the basis, the weaker the local physical price in relation to the futures exchange.

So it becomes important to have a knowledge of the basis to be able to translate a given futures price into a probable price for local delivery. The energy producer must understand that a "short" futures position (selling futures contracts) creates a "long" basis position.

The energy producer who sells futures contracts retains ownership of the physical product in the local market. If the local market increases in value and the futures market declines, the producer benefits from both positions. The futures industry translation of this event is that the basis strengthened. As a result, the producer benefits by being long the basis.

For a short (sell) hedger protecting against price declines
- a strengthening basis produces a profit

- a weakening basis produces a loss
- therefore, the short hedger is long the basis

Conversely, if the physical market declines and the futures market rises, the producer is harmed by both positions. The futures shorthand is that the basis weakened. As a result, the producer loses by being long the basis.

If a short (sell) futures position creates a long basis position for a hedger, then a long (buy) futures position creates a short basis position.

The energy end user that buys futures contracts in lieu of buying the physical product must, at a later date, buy the physical product and liquidate the futures position. The end-user is short the physical product until it is purchased for delivery in the local area. If the local market rises while the futures market declines, the end user is harmed by both positions.

Again, the futures terminology is that the basis strengthened. As a result, the end user loses by being short the basis.

For a long (buy) hedger, protecting against price increases

- a strengthening basis produces a loss
- a weakening basis produces a profit
- therefore, the long hedger is short the basis

But if the futures market rises while the physical market falls, the end user benefits from both positions. The futures market vernacular is that the basis weakened. And the end-user benefits by being short the basis.

BASIS AND DELIVERIES

A thorough knowledge of basis is essential to an understanding of the arbitrage opportunities that may exist with deliveries.

A delivery in futures is the tendering and receipt of a physical commodity to satisfy a futures contract obligation. Deliveries are an essential option that facilitates convergence of cash and futures prices at the expiry of the spot (nearby) futures contract. Liquidation of any open futures positions prior to the contract's expiration will preclude the necessity of making or taking delivery.

Although typically fewer than 3% of all futures contracts initiated result in delivery of the actual commodity, the provisions for delivery are very important to the function of the futures contracts. If there were no provisions for efficient delivery of commodities under futures contracts, futures prices would have little economic relationship to cash prices. However, the farther the cash commodity is from the point of delivery, the greater the volatility of the cash/futures relationship.

An excellent example, demonstrating that basis can be a market in and of itself, is that of natural gas in western North America.

In order for your local cash price to be accepted as a hedge for auditing purposes, General Accepted Accounting Procedures (GAAP) require that it must correlate with the futures price at least 80% of the time that the hedge is in place. If there is less than 80% correlation, the futures position cannot be accounted for as a bona fide commercial hedge.

From the minute that natural gas began trading on the NYMEX, western U.S. and Canadian gas markets had little correlation with the Henry Hub delivery mechanism of the NYMEX Natural Gas Futures Contract. (The Henry Hub is served by Gulf Coast and Mid-continent gas producers and delivers to markets in the Midwest and Northeast.) The Kansas City Board of Trade became sensitive to the needs of the Western markets and responded with the Western Natural Gas Futures and Options Contract. This began trading August 5, 1995, with a Permian Basin Waha, Texas delivery mechanism.

This new contract soon proved to be a much more favorable correlation that the Henry Hub delivery mechanism for correlation purposes. Thus, one can begin to appreciate the importance of basis trading.

APPENDIX V. THE MILESTONES

1821. Virginia gunsmith Aaron Hart accidentally drills first natural gas well on the
continent and deliberately builds first natural gas pipeline.

1859. Col. Edwin Drake discovers oil in Venango County, Pennsylvania, at a depth of 69 1/2 feet.

1866. First oil well drilled in Texas, in Nacogdoches County.

1897. April. Nellie Johnstone No. 1 completed, becoming the first commercial oil well in Oklahoma.

1901. Discovery of Spindletop Field in Texas. Drilling mud used for the first time in drilling of Spindletop wells. Price of oil falls dramatically.

1901. First oil production in Louisiana from Heywood Brothers No. 1 Jennings in Acadia Parish.

1905. Glenn Pool Field discovered near Tulsa, Oklahoma.

1908. First oil production in Middle East at Masjid-i Suleiman, Iran.

1911. Sherman Act's antitrust legislation used as basis for breaking up Standard Oil Trust.

1918. American Gas Association (AGA) founded.

1919. American Petroleum Institute (API) founded.

1923. National Association of Railway Commissioners, founded in 1889, becomes National Association of Regulatory Utility Commissioners (NARUC).

1929. Independent Petroleum Association of America (IPAA) founded.

1930, October. No. 3 Daisy Bradford well discovers East Texas Field.

1933. Edison Electric Institute, trade association of the large natural gas and electric utilities, founded.

1935. Public Utility Holding Company Act (PUHCA) places financial dealings of utility holding companies under jurisdiction of Securities and Exchange Commission (SEC), to protect utility stock holders and consumers from potential abuses.

1936. First recorded crude oil production in Saudi Arabia.

1938. Mexico nationalizes (i.e., seizes) foreign oil companies.

1938. Natural Gas Act (NGA) places transportation and sale of natural gas in interstate commerce–that is, the pipelines–under jurisdiction of Federal Power Commission.

1944. Interstate Natural Gas Association of America (INGAA) founded.

1946. First recorded crude oil production in Kuwait.

1955, December. Rig count (number of drilling rigs at work) reaches 3,137–a record not broken until 1980.

1958. First commercial crude oil production in Alaska.

1960. Organization of Petroleum Exporting Countries (OPEC) is formed.

1964, November. United Kingdom grants licenses for exploration in North Sea.

1967. Natural Gas Supply Association (NGSA) founded.

1970, August. West Ekofisk oilfield discovered in Norwegian North Sea.

1972, August. Brent oilfield discovered in U.K. North Sea.

1973, October. OPEC increases prices by some 70%. Arab mem bers of OPEC cut production and announce embargo on sales to United States.

1974, OPEC crude postings increase by up to 130%.

1974, January. Construction permit for Alaskan Pipeline issued.

1974, March. OPEC embargo on oil sales to U.S. lifted.

1974, April. Bertha Rogers No. 1 completed near Washita, Oklahoma–at 31,441 feet, the deepest well drilled in U.S.

1974, November. International Energy Agency (IEA) formed.

1975. OPEC increased marker crude postings by 10%.

1975, May. Brae Field discovered in U.K. North Sea.

1975, September. IEA member nations agree to increase emer gency oil stocks to 70 days' supply from previous level of 60 days.

1975, December. Authorization of construction and filling of Strategic Petroleum Reserve.

1976, February. Design and implementation of two-tier pricing system for U.S. crude oil.

1976, Gas Research Institute (GRI) founded.

1977. Federal Energy Regulatory Commission (FERC) replaces Federal Power Commission. FERC formed to regulate, among other things, interstate wholesale sales and transportation of gas at "just and reasonable" rates.

1977, January. Saudi Arabia and United Arab Emirates increase prices by 5% while all other OPEC members increase prices by 10%.

1977, August. Start of North Slope production in Alaska.

1977, October. First crude oil imported for Strategic Petroleum Reserve.

1978. U.S. oil demand peaks at 18.847 million barrels per day.

1978. Heating oil futures begin trading on the New York Mercantile Exchange (NYMEX).

1978. Public Utility Regulatory Policies Act (PURPA) passed to encourage small-scale cogeneration and renewable resources, and apply a measure of competitive pressure on utilities to better con trol their generating costs.

1978, October. Iran's production levels are disrupted by political/religious turmoil.

1978, November. Natural Gas Policy Act (NGPA) places controls on natural gas prices and gives Federal Energy Regulatory Com mission (FERC) authority over intrastate as well as interstate gas pro duction.

1979. World oil demand peaks at 41.6 million barrels per day.

1979, May. Gasoline shortages and rationing in U.S.

1979, November. Official price of Saudi Light crude reacher $24 per barrel (bbl)

1980, April. President Carter signs the so-called Windfall Profits tax bill.

1980, May. Saudi Arabia raises price of Arabian Light to $28/bbl.

1980 June. OPEC meeting sets a $32/bbl. benchmark price with maximum price of $37/bbl.

1980 September. Iran-Iraq war disrupts production in both countries.

1980, December. OPEC meeting raises maximum price to $41/bbl. Saudi Arabia raises price for Arabian Light to $32/bbl.

1981, January. President Reagan lifts remaining price controls from domestic crude oil.

1981, March. U.S. crude oil wellhead price peaks at $34.70/bbl.

1981, May. OPEC decides to maintain current price levels, but most countries agree to cut production by 10% to firm sliding prices.

1981, October. OPEC set crude oil marker price at $34/bbl. Saudi Arabia puts production ceiling of 8.5 million bbl/day on Aramco crude.

1981, December. U.S. rig count peaks at 4,530 active rigs.

1982, March. OPEC imposes crude oil production ceiling of 17.5 million bbl/day in effort to firm falling prices.

1982, July. Federal regulators close Penn Square Bank, setting off domino effect among energy lending banks.

1982, December. OPEC agrees to 18.5-million bbl/day production ceiling for 1983.

1983. Crude oil futures begin trading on NYMEX.

1983, February. OPEC reduces production ceiling to 17.5 million bbl/day. Market crude price reduced to $29/bbl.

1984. Federal government bails out Continental llinois, in effect nationalizing the bank, to prevent another Penn-Square-Bank panic.

1984. Unleaded gasoline futures begin trading on NYMEX.

1984, October. OPEC cuts production ceiling to 16.0 million bbl/day. Marker crude remains at $29/bbl.

1985, January. Saudi Light price reduced to $28/bbl.

1985, January. Many U.S. natural gas prices decontrolled. The NGPA's "old" gas category remains under price controls.

1985, March. Coal miners in U.K. strike, causing serious effect on European energy demand.

1985, October. FERC issues Order 436, mandating open access on interstate pipelines, effectively beginning move toward pipelines as providers of transportation services.

1985, December. OPEC changes policy, will secure market share rather than support price.

1986, July. Average U.S. crude oil wellhead price bottoms out at $9.39/bbl, lowest price since November 1978. Posted price for West Texas Intermediate hits low of $12.25/bbl. U.S. rig count reaches new post-WWII low of 663.

1986, September. Prices begin firming after OPEC agrees to informal quota system for production.

1986, December. U.S. crude oil production falls to 8.35 million bbl/day, lowest figure since 1977.

1986, December. OPEC agrees to formal quota of 15.8 million bbl/day for first half of 1987.

1987. Propane futures begin trading on NYMEX.

1987, July. OPEC revises its crude oil production quota upward, to 16.6 million bbl/day.

1987, August. Posted price for West Texas Intermediate (U.S. benchmark crude) rebounds to $20/bbl. for short period before falling off again.

1988, August. Cease-fire between Iran and Iraq.

1988, October. Average price for world export crudes falls to $10.13/bbl.

1988, November. OPEC adopts new production quota of 18.5 million bbl/day for first half of 1989.

1988. U.S. imports of crude oil and petroleum products reach highest levels since 1979: 7.351 million bbl/day.

1989, July. Natural Gas Wellhead Decontrol Act sets schedule for final phase-out of wellhead price controls by January 1, 1993.

1989, March. Oil tanker *Exxon Valdez* runs aground off Alaska, causing largest U.S. oil spill.

1989, July. OPEC boosts production quota to 19.5 million bbl/day.

1989, October. OPEC raises production quota again, to 20.5 mil lion bbl/day.

1989. Average price of world export crude oil moves up to 20.7%, for an average of $16.65 bbl for the year. And OPEC production moves up to average 22.048 million bbl/day, highest level since 1981.

1989. U.S. crude oil production falls to 7.613 million bbl/day, lowest level since 1963.

1990, January. OPEC raises production quota to 22.1 million bbl/day.

1990, April. Natural gas futures begin trading on NYMEX.

1990, July. OPEC raises production quota again, to 22.5 million bbl/day.

1990, August. Iraq invades Kuwait. UN places embargo on export of Iraq crude oil.

1990, October. Spot price for West Texas Intermediate hits $36.09/bbl.

1990, December. Saudi Arabia boosts production to 8.3 million bbl/day to make up for lost output from Iraq and Kuwait.

1991, January. UN forces engage Iraq, oust its army from Kuwait. UN embargo in Iraq crude exports remains in place.

1991, April. OPEC lowers production quota to 22.3 million bbl/day.

1991, August. Declining CIS (former USSR) production falls below 10 million bbl/day, lowest production since 1975.

1991, October. OPEC raises production quota to all-time high: 23.7 million bbl/day.

1992. FERC issues Order 636 (the so-called Mega-NOPR), "unbundling" all pipeline services, reducing role of interstate pipelines to that of carriers.

1992. Passage of the Energy Policy Act (EPAct) removes barriers to competition resulting from the PUHCA. FERC is empowered to order electric utilities to provide other power suppliers with access to their transmission facilities.

1992, January. Baker Hughes' 1991 average U.S. rig count at 860, lowest since 1942.

1992, July. Russian Republic's first-half oil production reported to have fallen by 950,000 from comparable period the year prior, averaging 9.5 million bbl/day.

1992, August. Hurricane Andrew sweeps across Gulf of Mexico with winds measured up to 260 mph, damaging drilling, production and other equipment and forcing Gulf Coast refineries to shut down.

1992, September. OPEC raises production quota to new all-time high: 24.2 million bbl/day.

1992, October. Average spot gas prices hit seven-year high of $2.57/Mcf.

1992, November. Ecuador withdraws from OPEC to avoid pro duction quotas and membership costs.

1992, December. Greek tanker *Aegean Sea* runs aground at harbor entrance of La Coruña, Spain, spilling estimated 490,000 bbl of crude.

1993, January. Baker Hughes U.S. rig count averaged 721 in 1992, lowest yearly average in more than 50 years.

1993, February. OPEC lowers production quota for second quar ter by 1 million bbl/day to 23.582 million bbl/day.

1993, April. President Clinton pledges to reduce carbon emissions from combustion of fossil fuels to 1990 levels by 2000.

1993, May. Canada approves North American Free Trade Agree ment (NAFTA) to improve trade among Canada, Mexico, and U.S.

1993, June. OPEC production quota increases to 24.14 million bbl/day due to increase in Kuwait's levels.

1993, July. NYMEX crude price sinks below $18/bbl at news UN might lift embargo on Iraqi exports.

1993, August. Chevron makes its first lifting of Point Arguello crude at Gaviota marine terminal in California following four years of controversy over tankering.

1993, September. OPEC sets fourth-quarter quota at 24.5 million bbl/day.

1993, October. FERC meets its goal of restructuring gas pipeline rates under Order 636 before heating season.

1993. North Sea production hits record high: 4.94 million bbl/day.

1993, November. Oil prices fall to lowest levels since pre-1990 Gulf crisis.

1993, November. U.S. approves NAFTA.

1993, December. NYMEX crude price drops to $14.57/bbl on Dec. 3, lowest level since Nov. 23, 1988, and Brent crude hits five-year low at $13.27/bbl.

1993, December. NYMEX gas price drops below $2/MMBTU.

1994, February. U.S. lifts trade embargo on Vietnam.

1994, April. NYMEX crude price exceeds $17/bbl on April 22, for first time since November 1993.

1994, May. FERC deregulates gas gathering in U.S.

1994, May. China bans imports of most crude oil and refined products.

1994, May. Cuba's first offshore oil strike occurs in Bay of Cardenas.

1994, June. NYMEX crude price exceeds $20/bbl.

1994, June. The EPA issues rule mandating that 30% of oxygenates required in reformulated gasoline come from renewable sources like ethanol.

1994, July. U.S. demand for first half of year increases by its largest margin in 8 years: 4.2% to 17.6 million bbl/day.

1994, August. U.S. natural gas wellhead price drops to $1.48/Mcf, lowest price since May 1992.

1994, September. California bans oil and gas leasing in state waters.

1994, October. North Sea production reaches record high: 5.76 million bbl/day.

1994, December. U.S. average crude production for the year at 6.662 million bbl/day, its lowest level since 1955.

1994, December. U.S. natural gas production for the year at 19.773 Tcf, continuing its increase since 1982.

1994, December. North Sea crude production hits record levels at 5.665 million bbl/day. United Kingdom reports 2.705 million bbl/day; Norway averages 2.811 million bbl/day.

1995, January. North Sea natural gas production hits high of 413.8 Bcf. United Kingdom reports 298 Bcf; Norway, 97 Bcf.

1995, January. Mandates for reformulated gasoline take effect in U.S. areas not complying with federal ozone pollution standards.

1995, March. FERC issues Notice of Proposed Rulemaking (NOPR) that it is considering universal open access to electric transmission grid.

1995, March. Equatorial Guinea gets first significant oil discovery.

1995, May. President Clinton orders halt to all U.S. trade with Iran.

1995, May. California Public Utilities Commission issues proposal for comment that would provide California electric customers direct access through wholesale power pool.

1995, June. OPEC production quota remains at 24.5 million bbl/day although actual production was 1.2 million bbl/day over quota.

1995, August. Kansas City Board of Trade's Western Natural Gas Futures & Options Contract begins.

1995, October. U.S. crude production averages 6.55 million bbl/day in first 9 months, lowest period average since 1954.

1995, November. Reed Tool's annual census of U.S. available rotary drilling rigs at its lowest level since WWII: 1,729 units.

1995, November. President Clinton signs into law bill granting royalty relief on production from deepwater federal tracts.

1995, December. NYMEX natural gas price sets record high on Dec. 19 at $2.868/MMBTU and hits $3.72/MMBTU on Dec. 21.

1996, March. Electricity futures contract begins trading on NYMEX, with deliveries at California-Oregon border and at Palo Verde, Arizona.

1996, April. FERC issues Order 888, opening electric transmission grid.

1996, April. Spurred by Deepwater Royalty Relief Act, Minerals Management Service Sale 157 in Gulf of Mexico sets records for number of bids offered and of tracts receiving bids.

1996, April. President Clinton lifts 23-year-old ban on export of crude from Alaska's North Slope.

1996, April. Japan lets long-standing law limiting imports of petroleum products expire, opening markets to competition.

1996, June. Gabon withdraws from OPEC.

1996, June. OPEC raises production quota to 25 million bbl/day.

1996, September. Outer Continental Shelf Lease Sale 161 brings more bids than any sale in western Gulf of Mexico and doubles amount of acreage available for drilling western Gulf.

1996, November. OPEC extends 25 million bbl/day quota to June 1997.

1996, December. Iraq resumes exports of oil to raise money for allegedly humanitarian purposes.

1996, December. Light sweet crude oil spot price reaches $28.10, highest price since January 1991. Natural gas closing futures price for contracts one month ahead reaches $4.573/MMBTU.

1997, June. OPEC production quotas set at 25.033 million bbl/day for another half-year. Actual production is near 27 million bbl/day.

Sources: Three-fourths of the material in this appendix is to be found *in The Oil & Gas Journal Energy Database* (Tulsa, Oklahoma, 800-752-9764). Secondary sources are: *Natural Gas Desk Book–Natural Gas as a Second Language,* prepared by Mobil, and *Natural Gas Intelligence's Natural Gas Glossary,* prepared by Sarah McKinley.

Energy Conversion Table (Based on Averages)

1 barrel of crude oil (42 gallons) equals:
5.8 million BTUs
5,604 cubic feet of natural gas
0.22 tons of bituminous coal
1,700 kilowatt hours of electricity

One short ton (2,000 lbs.) of bituminous coal equals:
26.2 million BTUs
4.52 barrels of oil
25,314 cubic feet of natural gas
7,679 kilowatt hours of electricity

1 cubic foot of natural gas equals:
1,032 BTUs
.000178 barrels of oil
.000040 tons of bituminous coal
0.30 kilowatt hours of electricity

1 kilowatt hour equals:
3,412 BTUs
.000588 barrels of oil
3.306 cubic feet of gas
.000013 tons of bituminous coal

Source: *Natural Gas Intelligence's Natural Gas Glossary*, prepared by Sarah McKinley.

INDEX

A

A.T. Kearney   117

Alaska Natural Wildlife Reserve (ANWR)   89

American Wind Energy Association   67

Analyst, corporate   xviii, 44, 51, 94,119

Andersen Consulting   117

Andersen, Svein S., and Oystein Noreng, Centre for Energy Studies, Norwegian School of Management   13

Apache Corp.   90

Arthur D. Little   117

Augustine, Norman   66, 69

B

BJ Services   96

BTU Man   consumer characteristics   xv, xix, 13, 16, 33; birth and development of   27-28;   disease   29-31, 35-36, 136, 137, 142; market signals   29-31

BTU marketer   15-19. Also see Re-Marketer.

BTU merchants   68, 71-82

BTU value stream   ix, xvi, 12, 15, 27, 39, 140-141

BTU World   x, xix, 74, 117, 119-121

Baby Boomers   142

Bailouts, S&Ls   20; Continental Illinois   101-102

Bain & Co.   117

Baker Hughes   96

Bank examiners   78, 100

Bankers, investment   113-121

Banks' regulatory restraints   61

Banks' relationship with oilpatch   77-78, 96-97, 99-102

Barings Bank   xviii, 76, 104, 108

Barrel (oil)   12, 147-148

Basis   79-81, 155-158

Bauch, William   xiii

Beck, Bob   xiii

C

E

H

I

M

Mcf (natural gas)   149-152

MacAvoy, Paul W.   53

Majors (vertically integrated oil and gas companies)   83-84, 87, 90, 95, 120

Management, senior   xviii, 49-55, 76-77, 102-109. Also see Boards of directors and CEOs.

Marketers   16-18, 28, 85, 138. Also see BTU marketer and Re-Marketer.

Marx, Groucho   143

McGill, Stuart   102-103

McKinsey & C.   53, 117

Melville, Herman (initial chapter quote)   123

Mercer Management Consulting   117

Merrill Lynch   16, 97

Mesa Petroleum   44

Metallgesellschaft of Germany   78

Michigan National Bank of Lansing   99

Midstream sector   11, 93-97, 104

Migration path   xviii, 28, 93-95, 105, 117

Milner, Carlos E., Jr.   xiii

Mineral ownership   85-86

Mitsubishi   78

Money managers   49-55

Money-making machine, the   54, 64

Monopoly(ies)   xv, xvii, 3-4, 7, 28, 62, 66-67, 135; natural monopoly(ies)   34, 66

Murkowski, Frank, U.S. Senator   22

N

NGC Corp.   6, 14

Napoleon   133

National Association of Corporate Directors   52

Natural gas   xv, xviii, 149-150

Natural gas contract. NYMEX, 158; Western, vii

Natural gas industry, natural gas deregulation   x, xi, xv, 4-6, 39, 54, 79

O

P

S

T

It's easy to do the right thing.

CCC makes it simple, efficient, and cost-effective to comply with U.S. copyright law. Through our collective licensing systems, you have lawful access to more than 1.7 million titles from over 9,000 publishers. Whether it's photocopying, electronic use, or the emerging information technologies of tomorrow—CCC makes it easy.

Call 1-800-982-3887 ext. 700 to find out how CCC can help you to Copy Right!^{SM}

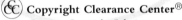 **Copyright Clearance Center**®
Creating Copyright Solutions

222 Rosewood Drive
Danvers, MA 01923